PROGRAM DEVELOPMENT INSTITUTE

INSTITUTE

PROGRAM DEVELOPMENT INSTITUTE

A TRAINING WITHIN INDUSTRY PROGRAM

Training Within Industry's Program Development Institute was provided in order to give training and analysis of production problems and planning of training to meet plant needs.

The training required five days and was given to groups of ten plant representatives to whom had been assigned functional responsibility for training.

WAR MANPOWER COMMISSION

Bureau of Training

Training Within Industry Service

1945

Originally published as *Program Development Institute*, released in 1945 by the War Manpower Commission of the Bureau of Training, Washington, District of Columbia.

Enna Products
1602 Carolina St.
Suite B3
Bellingham, WA 98229
Telephone: (360) 306-5369
Fax: (905) 481-0756
E-mail: info@enna.com

Cover Design/Illustrations by Khemanand Shiwram
Editor: Collin McLoughlin
Associate Editor: Shawna Gilleland

Library of Congress Control Number: 2009938940

Library of Congress Cataloging-in-Publication Data

United States. Bureau of Training. War Manpower Commission. 1945
    Program Development Institute

    ISBN 978-1-897363-96-6
    1. Training Within Industry   2. Training of employees 3. Organizational change
4. Productivity–Increasing through training   I. Title

Dedicated to the men and women of The Greatest Generation.

June 1, 1945.

To The Program Development Institute Conductor:

Your work in helping plant representatives to acquire the skill of meeting production problems through training can affect every person in the plants represented and presents the opportunity of helping to overcome production interferences which are critical in the war effort.

The developing of training plans to meet the plant's own specific needs is an in-plant job—no outsider can know the underlying causes of production problems. Each plant should have a designer of training. In some plants he will have a training title but he will not in others. The only important thing is that he have functional responsibility for the planning of training to meet production problems. It is your responsibility to (1) see that the right man is selected for the Institute, (2) that management understands the objective of the Program Development Institute, and (3) to give this man an opportunity to acquire this skill.

Each Program Development Institute presents a challenge—you as Institute Conductor must <u>instruct</u> the members, stimulate them to <u>practice, observe</u> their work, and <u>put them on their own</u> before the Institute closes. Your objective is to help the plant man to acquire this important skill, and to get during the Institute a start which will have results so convincing that continuing use of the method in his plan is assured.

Sincerely,

C. R. Dooley

C. R. Dooley, Director,

Training Within Industry Service.

CONTENTS

References

Materials

First Day — Problem Sheet and Definition of Terms
Cost Records Problem
Program Development 4-Step Card
Work Sheet for Step 1
Work Sheet for Step 2
Disinfectant Reprocessing Problem
Defective Hydraulics Problem
How Training can Be Done—Methods and Aids
How to Get a Plant Training Plan into Action
How to Get Continuing Results from Plant Training Programs

Second Day — Introducing the New Employee to the Job
Induction Plan Step 2 Work Sheets

Third Day — Management and Skills Supervision
Improving Supervisors' Knowledge of the Work
Keeping Supervisors Informed about Their Responsibilities

Fourth Day — How to Select New Supervisors

PROGRAM DEVELOPMENT INSTITUTE TIME SCHEDULE

First Day		First Day
25 min.	Introduction and Plan of Institute	
20 min.	Definition of Terms	
15 min.	Management chart	
10 min.	Problem Sheet	2 hours
5 min.	4-Step Method	55 min.
10 min.	Intermission	
1 hr. 30 min.	Application of Method—Cost Records Problem	
1 hr.	Importance of evidence and training action, and	
	2 drill problems on Step 1, 1 group, 1 individual	
1 hr.	Method and Aids and 2 drill problems on Step 2	3 hours
10 min.	Intermission	30 min.
1 hr.	Getting a Plan into Action, and 2 drill problems on Steps 3 and 4	
20 min.	Assignment for second day	

Second Day		Second Day
10 min.	4-Step Method	3 hours
2 hr. 50 min.	3 Assigned Problems (10 min. intermission included)	
1 hr. 30 min.	Induction	
10 min.	Intermission	3 hours
2 hrs.	3 Assigned Problems	45 min.
5 min.	Schedule for Third Day	

Third Day		Third Day
2 hrs.	3 Assigned Problems	2 hours
10 min.	Intermission	55 min.
45 min.	W.M.C. Training Services	
30 min.	Plant Meetings	
40 min.	1 Assigned Problem	1 hour
45 min.	Assignment for remainder of Institute	55 min.

Fourth Day		Fourth Day
20 min.	Difference between problems, programs and plans	
2 hr. 40 min.	3 Plans (10 min. intermission included)	3 hours
1 hr.	Selecting supervisors	3 hours
2 hr. 40 min.	3 Plans (10 min. intermission included)	40 min.

Fifth Day		Fifth Day
1 hr. 40 min.	2 Plans	
10 min.	Intermission	
20 min.	Checking Results	3 hours
50 min.	1 Plan	
50 min.	1 Plan	
10 min.	Relation of Plans and Programs	
10 min.	Intermission	not more
1 hr.	1 Plan	than 2 hrs.
45 min.	Summary	55 min.

	Purpose	Emphasis
FIRST DAY MORNING	To establish that the Institute is designed to give members practice in using the 4-Step Method in the Institute and in their own plants and to illustrate the method by application in a problem presented by the Institute Conductor.	Training must be designed to meet specific production problems. This is in-plant, on-the-job work. Details of a training plan are determined by analyzing evidence of the problem.
AFTERNOON	To familiarize members with use of work sheets through practice on drill problems and to show relation of steps.	All four steps are necessary in order to meet a production problem through training.
SECOND DAY MORNING	To get practice, skill, and conviction through use of method by each member on a standardized problem.	Training cannot be planned in an Institute, but understanding of method can be acquired through practice.
AFTERNOON	To present information about characteristics of successful induction plans. To continue practice on assigned problems.	Induction must be planned specifically for each plant.
THIRD DAY MORNING	To continue practice on assigned problems. To outline W.M.C. training services.	Detail is needed in both evidence and content. Public agencies give some assistance in meeting plant needs.
AFTERNOON	To establish key points of effective meetings. To continue practice on assigned problems. To outline members' use of method in own plants.	Each member is to make complete 4-Step plan for own plant. Meetings are depended on in-plant training programs.
FOURTH DAY MORNING	To have two plans presented. To give each member opportunity to improve own plan on basis of group discussion of methods.	Evidence of the production problem must be met by the plan. Only member presenting plan has facts about evidence in his plant.
AFTERNOON	To present T.W.I. plan for supervisory selection. To have three plans presented.	Training director is concerned with caliber of supervision.
FIFTH DAY MORNING	To emphasize importance of checking results, and to consider evaluation techniques. To have three plans presented.	Results are checked against evidence of need—Is the production problem being met through training? Training plan must include Step 4.
AFTERNOON	To have two plans presented. To stress importance of relation of any training plan to other plans and programs. To stress line and staff responsibility. To get conviction of value of 4-Step Method.	Program Development skill is acquired through use of method. Timing and need must be considered before plan is scheduled. Staff provides technical "know-how." Use of method will help meet production problems through training.

CODE

CAPITALS . . . . Section Heads

Horizontal line across page . . . . Encloses section for timing

Plain type . . . . Trainer says in own words

★   Star in front of line . . . . Trainer says verbatim

Material between lines . . . . Board Work

Bracket . . . . Instruction to trainer

FIRST DAY - MORNING

*Allow
25 min*

OPENING THE INSTITUTE

District Representative welcomes Institute members, introduces himself and the Institute Conductor—not more than 5 minutes.

Institute Conductor acknowledges introduction.

1. Let's get an idea of who's here.

   Use name cards if appropriate.

Ask each man to tell his position, to whom he reports, size of his plant (now—before the war—what it may be a year from now), whether plant is making new product, etc.

All of you have a <u>responsibility</u> for organizing and coordinating training to meet production problems. You are <u>not trainers</u>. You <u>plan training</u>, see that it gets done, and check results.

★ 2. In this Institute we are going to work on how to meet a
★ production problem through training.
★ This is not a meeting. It is a work session; we will learn
★ by doing.
★ You have been assigned the responsibility for developing
★ training plans in your plant.
★ Your managements have sent you here. They will review
★ with you the plan you develop.

Write across top
of blackboard:

How to Meet a Production Problem
Through Training

3. This Program Development Institute requires five days:

the first three, today and the next two days
the last two on _____ and _____ .

Between this section of the Institute and the time when we reconvene, you will spend considerable time in your own plant, planning to meet a current production problem through training.

When we all return on _____ we will take up, individually, the training plan each of you prepares to meet a problem of your own plant.

1

25 min
to here If Institute time has not been cleared for all members, take up individually during intermission.

Allow
20 min.

DEFINITION OF TERMS

Just to keep straight—to see that we have the same meaning for the terms—lets agree on some we will be using all the time. First, lets make sure we all have the same understanding for what we have on the board—"How to Meet a Production Problem Training.

Do <u>not</u> ask what production means. Give definition. Discuss the definitions until each member of the group understands them all. Get acceptance. Put on board briefly. Follow same procedure for each. Tell members they will not need to write them down, that you have copies.

★ 1. By production we mean the end result—the product or
★ service.

What is production in the organization which sent you here?

Ask each member.

For a man sent by a plant, it is the end product of the plant.

A man who represents just a department of a plant is concerned with the finished work of that department—perhaps a sub-assembly.

In a non-manufacturing company or department, production may be something like "passenger railroad transportation" or "bills for electric current."

By production we mean:

Write on board:

> **What is Production?**
> End result — product or service — of an organization, plant, department, or unit.

★ 2. By a "production problem" we mean anything that keeps
★ us from getting out the work for which our organization
★ exists.

2

What is a Production Problem?
Anything which interferes with production

Scrap is a common production problem.

We uncover some production problems and try to <u>correct</u> or <u>improve</u> them. Others can be anticipated and we may <u>prevent</u> them.

In your plants there are problems that interfere with getting out your work of _____ and _____. You are going to work on solving those problems.

3. Training is <u>a</u> way to solve <u>a</u> production problem.

Write on board:

What is Training?
<u>A</u> way to solve <u>a</u> production problem.

There are many ways to solve production problems. Engineers attack those involving machines, and metallurgists and chemists work on materials.

Training deals with people.

You will notice that we say <u>a</u> way—not the only way.

And that we say <u>a</u> production problem—you have to tackle one at a time.

Training is <u>a</u> way to solve a problem of scrap.

4. There are different causes for scrap. Several kinds of training may be needed. In this Institute, we will say that a training plan is a way to get at a specific part of a specific production problem.

5. A training program is the organization of all the training plans stemming out of one production problem.

Write on board:

What is a Training Plan?
An organized method of solving a specific part of a production problem.

What is a Training Program?
A combination of training plans coordinated to meet the training needs cause by a specific production program.

This is all of the training plans connected with a particular scrap problem are the training program for that problem.

★ 6. All of you are here because you have functional
★ responsibility for training.

You have various titles in your own organizations. Some of you have full-time responsibility for training, some have other duties.

★ All of you are here for a common purpose—developing
★ and coordinating training plans and programs in order to
★ help management solve its production problem through
★ people.

★ 7. What is management?

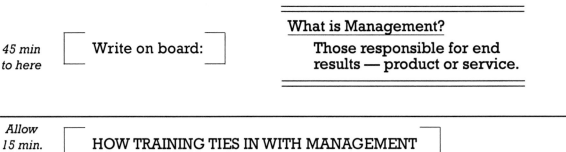

45 min to here

Write on board:

What is Management?

Those responsible for end results — product or service.

Allow 15 min.

HOW TRAINING TIES IN WITH MANAGEMENT

Now let's see where the training function fits into the management picture.

Erase all board work except slogan across top. Develop chart from bottom to top, and "Line" before "Staff," explaining the necessary variations which are caused by size of the business and the fact that one business is different from another. Do not connect staff positions to line organization—explain that the place each ties in is different in each plant.

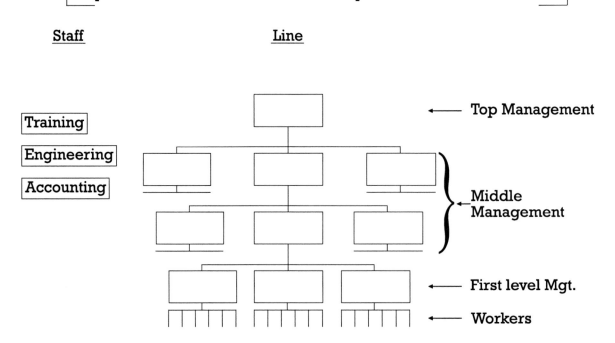

Staff — Training, Engineering, Accounting

Line — Top Management, Middle Management, First level Mgt., Workers

4

Use the following as ideas to discuss while you are working on the chart.

Line organization is responsible for the actual accomplishment of end results in terms of products or services. The staff—engineers, chemists, purchasing agents, personnel men, accountants, lawyers, training men—provide service to the line organization.

Talking about training as a staff service does not mean "a training staff." It does not always mean, in small plants for instance, that it even takes one man's full time.

1 hr. to here

2. Some of you hold positions in both the line and the staff. When you are planning training you are filling a staff responsibility, even if the line person you are assisting is yourself.

Allow 10 min.

PROBLEM SHEET

Each one of your plants is different.

Do you have any common problems?

Let's take a look at some common problems in plants. How about these on this sheet.

Distribute problem sheets. Announce that definitions are on other side.

Do you have any of these problems in your plant?

As soon as one member indicates his plant has a problem, ask:

Were people involved?

Could this problem be met through training?

Continue only until you have acceptance of the idea that the problem sheet represents common problems. Do not count "most common problems" or belabor the discussion.

Since several have the same problems, is there a possibility that just exactly the same approach can be used? No.

Training plans must be tailored for a particular plant.

Your problems will not be exactly alike—therefore, your plans to meet them cannot be exactly alike.

5

★ In this Institute we cannot decide what is needed in
★ any plant. <u>We</u> cannot plan training for <u>your</u> plant.

★ <u>Spotting production problems</u> and <u>developing training</u>
★ <u>plans are in-plant jobs.</u>

We are going to develop skill in using a 4-step method of meeting production problems through training.

1 hr.
10 min
to here

> Erase all board work except slogan.

Allow
5 min.

> THE 4-STEP METHOD

> Present—do not develop.

★ The first of the four steps of the Program Development
★ method is:

> Put on board,
> under slogan.

1. Spot a <u>production</u> problem.

★ One production problem may indicate that several training
★ plans are needed but we can only:

> Put on board next:

Tackle one specific need at a time.

★ Step 2 is:

> Put on board:

2. Develop a <u>specific</u> plan.

★ We have a caution with this step:

> Put on board:

Watch for relation of this plan
to other current training plans
and programs.

★ Step 3 is:

> Put on board:

3. Get plan into <u>action</u>.

★ It is very important to:

> Put on board:

Be sure management participates.

6

★ Step 4 is:

Put on board:

4. Check <u>results</u>.

★ And we end with what really counts:

1 hr.
15 min
to here

Put on board:

Is the plan helping production?

This is the method we are going to use.

Take 10 minute intermission here.

Allow
1 hr.
30 min.

DEMONSTRATE USE OF PROGRAM DEVELOPMENT 4-STEP METHOD THROUGH USE OF COST RECORDS PROBLEM.

1. Training as an everyday operating tool cannot be planned by any outsider.

But we can get an understanding of the <u>method</u> by looking at how one training director used it on a production problem in his plant.

2. Here is what one training director in a gear manufacturing plant faced. I will read this to you just as the training director wrote it down.

> Last Monday I went to the works manager's weekly meeting. The cost accountant and I were there, as well as the six superintendents. The works manager was all worked up about the cost records, and got pretty tough with the chief accountant. He asked, "How does it happen that those 50 men at double time, the Sunday after the breakdown in Department 2, didn't affect costs?
> That got me started on going over a lot of our cost records and you can't make me think our estimates are so good that every job hits the estimate—never over, never under."
>
> He went on to say, "Costs don't seem to mean a thing around this place. Do you think I'm going to wait for a government auditor to find what's wrong? And what kind of fix are we going to be in to go after business when the war's over? I want to know what's wrong, and I want it fixed up."

3. This works manager had a problem. Do you remember we said that we tried to <u>correct</u> or <u>improve</u> some conditions? That's what this works manager, this member of top management who was responsible for production, wanted. He was also trying to <u>anticipate</u> something that looked even worse. Now what was his production problem?

The cost accountant said this wasn't anything new—he'd questioned the superintendents' weekly reports before, and he didn't want the same old story—that they just made them up from the foremen's Daily Operating Reports.

The superintendents said they had never realized how their weekly reports tied in with the company's operations and profits. They said they had never made much of this point with the foremen.

The upshot was that the superintendents said they would get their foremen together so the cost accountant could discuss this cost record problem with them. I went to that meeting, too. Both the chief accountant and I learned some things there. A foreman has an estimated cost on each job in his department. If he's going to run over more than 5%, he has to get advance approval. It isn't hard to get, but it does take a lot of paper work.

If he saves time on one job, he can take care of running over on another. In that way, he can avoid asking for a change in the estimates. The cost accountant was horrified that they juggled costs like that.

Here's how it boiled down. A foreman may have 20 to 50 workers. Now each worker has a time card, and even the accountant agrees it is a very detailed and complicated card.

The time cards are a sore subject. Most of the time clocks are in out-of-the-way positions and the average is one clock for 200 people.

Well—nobody bothers filling in the job numbers on time cards. The foremen would just as soon not have them filled in—they mark them up after they see what labor costs they should charge, according to the estimate! The foremen spoke up and said they had never understood how important their Daily Operating Reports were.

Don't think they said all this without saying plenty about new time cards, moving the clocks, making it easier to revise estimates. The superintendents and the cost accountant answered quite a few questions. The cost information does have to be recorded. The plant cannot charge more than 5% over the estimate without getting the Army in on it.

As to the time clocks—we can't get any more, but we may be able to find better locations. Maybe the time card can be changed—but not overnight. I looked at some of the time cards and I know I'm really going to have to dig into this time card angle, too. But the cost records have to be corrected <u>right away</u>.

4. This plant <u>did</u> have a problem. The works manager realized that the company's position was questionable both on current government contracts and for its post-war business.

Now we are not going to concern ourselves whether this kind of mess <u>should</u> happen. It <u>did</u> happen.

1 hr.
45 min
to here

We will look at what can be done to solve the problem, using the Program Development 4-step method.

5. | Distribute cards individually. |

Let's look at these cards.

★ Step 1 is "Spot a Production Problem." We agreed that the
★ production problem is "Inaccurate cost records."

> In this case, the production problem was spotted by the works manager. Sometimes the training man will spot the problem, sometimes someone will call it to his attention.

> But even if it is called to his attention, as it was this time, the works manager rarely gives the training director enough information for him to actually plan the training needed. The training man has to dig into it himself.

| Refer to card. |

★ <u>Get supervisors and workers to tell about their</u>
★ <u>current problems.</u>

> Do we know something about this? The foremen felt they certainly had problems—those Daily Operating Reports were headaches.

> And the workers thought they had problems too. They didn't like the time cards and they didn't like the location of the time clock.

> So far the training director hasn't talked to the workers, but if or when he does, he'll probably hear a lot more.

★ <u>Uncover problems by reviewing records—performance,</u>
★ <u>cost, turnover, rejects, accidents.</u>

> This problem was uncovered when the works manager took a look at the cost records.

★ <u>Anticipate problems resulting from changes—</u>
★ <u>organization, production, or policies.</u>

The works manager in this problem was looking not only at the plant's current standing but at its competitive situation later.

★ Next we come to "<u>Analyze this evidence</u>," and after that we
★ find "<u>Identify training needed</u>" so that we can "<u>Tackle one</u>
★ <u>specific need at a time</u>."

★ Lets try to <u>analyze this evidence</u> so we can do just that.

★ Remember that all we are doing is <u>looking</u> at the 4-step
★ method. Only the person who knows all about this plant
★ is going to be able to solve its production problem.

★ But we can gain familiarity with the method by looking at
★ this sample problem. We can make sure that we all have a
★ common understanding of the method.

We will analyze the evidence we have in order to identify training needed.

Just to help you recall the evidence in this problem, here is a copy of it as read.

Distribute Cost Records problem.

Erase previous board work. See blackboard guide.

Put heading for evidence column on board.

Ask members for evidence, to suggest action, etc. Do not let this drag. It is <u>not</u> necessary to get these particular words on the board, or this order, but all material must be included. The Institute Conductor should use leading questions. Inquire what came out of the general superintendent's meeting. Use "What about the location of the time clock?"

Fill evidence column first. Then say, "We look at the evidence and ask 'Is any action needed? Specifically, is any <u>training ac-</u><u>tion needed?</u>' "

Fill in training column headings, and question the first item of evidence.

Ask "Is any other action needed?" Fill in column heading.

Take each item of evidence separately.

Make sure that training of foremen in how to make out D.O.R. is specifically mentioned. If necessary, say "This training director decided _____.

Do not erase any of this board work.

★ Since we can <u>tackle only one specific need at a time</u>, we
★ will take the training of foremen in how to make out the
★ Daily Operating Report.

10

What is the Production Problem? ___ Inaccurate Cost Records

EVIDENCE	TRAINING ACTION NEEDED		OTHER ACTION NEEDED
	Training for Whom?	Training in What?	
50 men Dept. 2 double time didn't affect cost records.	Foreman of Dept. 2	Accurate cost records	
Every cost report agrees with estimate			
Superintendent makes weekly report from D.O.R.'s			
Supts. didn't understand relation of costs to operations	Superintendents	Importance of cost records	
Cost accountant had complained before			
Advance approval to run more than 5% over estimate			
Estimate change procedure complicated	Foremen	How to change estimate	Simplify procedure?
Cost reports juggled to match estimates	Foremen	Importance of cost records	
Foremen make D.O.R.'s from estimate, not from time cards	Foremen	How to make out D.O.R.	
Foreman has 20-50 workers			
Time clock location bad			Move clock?
Time cards not filled in by workers	Workers	Importance of time cards	
Time cards complicated	Workers	How to fill time card	Simplify card?
Foreman doesn't require filling in time cards	Foremen	Importance of cost records	
Foreman fills time cards to match estimate	Foremen	Importance of cost records	
Foremen didn't understand relation of D.O.R.'s to operations	Foremen	Importance of D.O.R.	

"TACKLE ONE SPECIFIC NEED AT A TIME"

That is the only part of this problem we can tackle right now. The others depend on simplifying procedures, new time cards, etc.

But we can get started on how to fill out the D.O.R. right now.

We don't know enough about this plant and its cost procedures to know how much detail is necessary.

We do know that something has to be done right away to get accurate cost records every day.

*2 hrs.
5 min
to here*

Something can be done right away about the Daily Operating Report.

6. Step 2 is "Develop a Specific Plan."

Let's look at our cards.

What is the specific plan?—the "Daily Operating Report."

> This training director combined several items from Step 1.

Who will be trained?

> We said that the foremen had to be trained. There were 30 of them.

What content?

> We are going to have to consider two things—the foremen do not understand the importance or the use of their D.O.R.'s and they are not making them out properly. These points will have to be considered when we plan content.

Who can help determine?

> The training director certainly will need help in determining the content. Both production executives and a staff man, the chief accountant, are in on this.

How can it be done best? and Who should do the training?

> There are two quite different kinds of content involved.

(For use with Step 2 of P.D. Method - Use card)

What is the Specific Plan? ___ Daily Operating Report

Training for Whom? ___ Foremen   Training for How Many? __ 30

What Content?	How Can It Be Done Best?	Who Will Train or Help?	When? How Long?	Where?
1. Importance of D.O.R. Government audit Legal responsibility Prospective orders Post-war business	Personal appeal	General Superintendent	1/2 hour each group, all 3 groups, 10 each next Monday	General Superintendents office
2. Analysis of D.O.R. Use in making weekly report Errors and effect	Blow-up chart of weekly report, explanation, questions Sample sets of time cards, D.O.R.'s, weekly report, job cost report	Chief Accountant	2 hours each group, all on Tuesday	Conference room
3. Filling in D.O.R. Time card basis Charges to specific jobs Delay — charges to overhead Day work — how charged Job charges vs. estimates	Practice on simple material Analysis of own reports	Chief Accountant	2 hours each group, Wednesday	Conference room
Material charges			2 hours each group, Thursday	Conference room

What is the Relation of this Plan to Other Current Training Plans and Programs? ___ This is the most important problem in plant right now — this takes precedence over any other training program. This is only one part of the whole problem, but the only one we can get at immediately.

13

One is convincing the foremen that this is something important. We may need someone who carries a lot of weight to put this over.

Another is exactly how to fill out this report. Someone who really knows how to handle this report is going to have to do the instructing.

<u>When should it be done and how long will it take</u>?

We know that this is something that has to be done right away. Exactly how long it will take will depend on the specific content.

<u>Where should it be done</u>?

This depends on the plant and the facilities it has. Some training, by its very nature, has to be done where the equipment is—this is not that kind. What is required here is a place for the foremen to get together.

Step 2 ends with the warning, "<u>Watch for relation of this plan to other current training plans and programs</u>."

Sometimes a training plan just can't get started because the timing isn't right, because facilities and equipment are not ready, because there is no one available to do the training, or because people can't take time off from production.

Other times a new plan is so important that other training is delayed or stopped if necessary.

In any case, you have to consider what else is going on in the plant.

★ We are not going to be able to design this plant's training
★ plan, but we can see how this training director applied the
★ method.

See blackboard guide.

Put in content item 1; take it across work sheet, then 2, then 3.

<u>Present</u> this step—do not develop. Discuss and clarify, but keep on the basis of what this training director did.

Make sure group understands that <u>practice</u> is included because foremen are learning how to <u>do</u> something.

2 hrs. 25 min to here

Show how content ties back to evidence. Stress—training director <u>designed</u> plan but is not going to <u>train</u>.

Do not erase board work.

7. Now we are ready for Step 3—"Get Plan into Action."

> Work from card.

Often, in order to get support for a training plan, it is necessary to do some selling.

While the training man was handed the problem, he will still need to "Stress to management evidence of need"—in light of the facts and figures, he is going to have to sell the works manager on putting 195 hours of the foremen's time into this.

He has to sell the plan by which he expects to solve the problem, so he will "Present the expected results" and "Discuss plan—content and methods."

Management wants something done about this problem. To answer the question about when he's going to do something, he will "Submit timetable for plan."

Often it is necessary to "Train those who do the training." If someone who doesn't the know the Daily Operating Report is to do the training, he would need help, wouldn't he?

And if he knows the report, but doesn't know how to instruct, he'll need help.

The best plan fails if the instructor is not able to instruct.

The next point on our card is "Secure understanding and acceptance by those affected."

In this plant there is pretty strong feeling about those Daily Operating Reports. They are regarded as a nuisance—a necessary evil to be gotten rid of with as few headaches as possible.

The works manager is going to have to "Fix responsibilities for continuing use."

It's going to take some attention to get the foremen to understand why the plant needs accurate Daily Operating Reports.

The superintendents may have to do a lot of hammering to get old habits broken.

*2 hrs.
35 min
to here*

Step 3 ends with "Be sure management participates." We don't just mean "approves." Managers have to operate this plan as they do other plans dealing with production.

8. Step 4 on our card is "Check results."

It will be very easy to check results. They can be checked against the previous unsatisfactory conditions.

The "results that will be looked for" will be reports that give an

15

accurate report of production costs.

How will <u>management be informed</u>? Through the same reports which pointed out the problems in the first place. You don't have to set up elaborate new reports.

The training director is interested in something else besides results. He has to know "<u>Is the plan being followed</u>?"

If the plan isn't followed, and results are poor, that's one thing. If the plan is followed, and results are poor, that's another.

Some plans have to be <u>kept in use</u>—some have a specific, short-term purpose. This training director will help the superintendents to see that the foremen don't slip back into bad habits and that new men get off to the right start.

If the plan continues, if there is any change in plant procedure — such as new time cards—he will need to consider whether any <u>changes in the plan</u> are necessary.

Step 4 ends with "<u>Is the plan helping production</u>?" Do you remember why this was a production problem? In this case the management wants the present condition corrected and serious trouble prevented.

It is necessary for Step 4 to be worked out when the training man makes his plans.

9. At the end of our card is something the training man must not forget. <u>We put it there to remind you regularly.</u>

Read it aloud:

★ <u>Responsibility for Training Results.</u>

★ The LINE organization has the responsibility for making
★ continuing use of the knowledge and skills acquired
★ through training as a regular part of the operating job.

★ The STAFF provides plans and technical "know how" and
★ does the same things FOR but usually works THROUGH
★ the line it organization.

Tie back to line and staff chart.

2 hrs.
55 min
to here

10. We have taken a general look at the method applied to a sample problem. Are there any questions?

Before the session starts, Institute Conductor puts form for Work Sheet 1 on board, and for Work Sheet 2 on the reverse of other board.

*Allow
20 min*

IMPORTANCE OF EVIDENCE AND TRAINING ACTIONS

1. There are some tools—some work sheets—that we use in this 4-step method.

This afternoon we are going to learn to use those tools. We are not interested in the problems themselves, or the plans—just in the tools that make the method simpler.

First we'll look at Step 1.

Ask members to look at cards—have one read Step 1.

You will recall that we followed a definite pattern as we worked on the blackboard for Step 1 of the cost records problem this morning.

Here is a simple form similar to the one we have on the board, and which we used this morning.

Pass out supply of blank Step 1 Work Sheets.

Let's look it over to be certain we understand it.

Read first line under heading.

2. What is the Production Problem?

Review definitions of "production" and "production problems."

★ One way of spotting the production problem is to ask
★ ourselves what we are trying to:
★   correct,
★   improve, or
★   prevent.

This brings out:

- What is wrong—a production problem
- What is slow, wasteful or expensive—a production problem
- What could happen—a production problem

We are not trying to identify a <u>training</u> problem—it must be a <u>production</u> problem.

> Remind members of what a production problem really is—anything that interferes with production. Ask:

- What is wrong in the plant?
- What are you trying to stop?
- What does the boss want?
- What conditions does management want corrected or anticipated?

> Ask members for examples in their own plants—tie back to problem sheet if necessary.
>
> Be certain it is a <u>production</u> problem, not a <u>training</u> problem. Discuss until all are clear as to the difference.

3. Next we have the column headed <u>Evidence</u>.

This means facts and figures; underlying causes and conditions; what has to be corrected, improved, prevented.

In this column list <u>ALL</u> evidence available.

> We can determine much of it by using the first three subheads under Step 1 of the 4-step method.

> > Refer to card. Perhaps have a member read an item, then discuss and amplify it in terms of the types of plants represented in the group.

> Much of the evidence has to come from people in the line organization. The closer you are to the line, the better job you will do on getting evidence.

> The entries under evidence should be simply stated, but accurate, brief and clear. Get evidence in figures so you will have something concrete to check against when you check results.

> > Always exhaust all three sources of evidence (first three subheads of Step 1) before continuing with the problem.

It is only when we get at underlying causes, reasons, and related conditions that we really see what can be done about the problem.

Be certain everyone understands what is meant by EVIDENCE before you go on to the next column.

4. Next is a 2-part column headed TRAINING ACTION NEEDED.

That word "needed" is important. We are not interested in training that could be undertaken on a general basis—just on that which must be done.

The two parts are Training for Whom and Training in What.

Training for Whom means the actual people who will be trained. For example:

> Supervisors   Clerks
> Welders   Engineers
> Machinists   Department heads

Training in What means the specific knowledge or skill needed by any particular person, or what they need to know, or what they will have to learn to do.

The training is not planned here but needs are identified.

This is the place where you make notes about training action to overcame lacks, improve present performance, or head off future lacks.

Cite examples and have group contribute additional examples.

5. The last column is Other Action Needed.

Here may be listed suggestions for something other than training.

Anything which bears on the production problem but which is not accomplished through training—such as changing an accounting procedure or moving equipment.

Sometimes the "other action" must come before "training action." The training director usually can't take this "other action," but he will call attention to its importance.

You can't use this as an alibi. If there is some part of the problem which can be solved through training—get on it. Call attention to other action.

6. At the bottom of the work sheet is a very important line:
<u>Tackle one specific need at a time</u>.

How do you decide which training need to tackle first?

If members do not suggest these points, Institute Conductor makes them:

20 min
to here

neediest need	good field to make showing
easiest to sell	no delays for this plan
instructors ready	may not have to try others
fastest results	if this works

Allow
40 min

DRILL PROBLEMS FOR WORK SHEET NO. 1

1. Here is a sample problem which I'd like to tell you about.

Tell this problem as follows:

A spice company has a war contract for a powerful disinfectant. In order to keep it at full strength until it is used, it must get as little air as possible.

The packaging department has only one shift. There is a lot of waste because loose powder is left open at the end of the shift.

The powder can be reprocessed but the result is that only 80% of the production is packed the first time it's processed.

The supervisors don't seem to know how much disinfectant to have sent in—if the operators run out of powder, it means delay. So most of the supervisors order too much.

Everything in the plant is running very smoothly except for this problem. The only training going on at present is a course out of hours.

(For use with Step 1 of P.D. Method - Use card)

What is the Production Problem? _____ 20% reprocessing of disinfectant powder

| EVIDENCE | TRAINING ACTION NEEDED | | OTHER ACTION NEEDED |
	Training for Whom?	Training in What?	
Disinfectant must be protected from air	Supervisors	Properties of disinfectant	Closed hoppers?
Only 80% of production gets packed	Operators	Importance of this product	
Disinfectant left ope approximately 16 hours at end of shift in in packaging department	Supervisors	Estimating needs Disposal of excess	Return unpacked stock at end of shift?
Supervisors order too much disinfectant	Supervisors	Estimating needs	Scheduled deliveries?
Supervisors want to avoid delays in getting disinfectant			

"TACKLE ONE SPECIFIC NEED AT A TIME"

Let's get one thing straight. We are not "doing a Step 1" on this problem. We are just learning to use the work sheet you will use when you really go to work on a problem. We cannot determine underlying causes in a problem we know little about. But we can make sure we recognize an underlying cause.

Let's not worry about whether there is enough evidence. In just this much we have the full range of the evidence column.

We have some figures—only 80% of the disinfectant production goes directly into packages. Unpacked disinfectant is left open until the next day.

And it is a fact that this disinfectant must be protected from air so it will remain full strength.

Now what are the underlying causes? The supervisors order too much disinfectant because they don't want delays. They don't seem to be able to figure how much they really need.

What we have is not a complete Step 1—but do we understand the Step 1 work sheet?

2. Here is another problem—you, individually, will fill out a Step 1 work sheet just as we did together.

Planes are being rejected because of a specific defect in the hydraulic system. This happens in about one plane out of three. The people who are installing the hydraulic system are highly experienced workers.

The situation was bad enough that the superintendent took enough supervisors and inspectors to stay right with the men who were installing the hydraulic system. Nobody could find any faulty work. Yet one plane out of three had leaks by the time it got to final inspection.

Then they began to trace what happened after the hydraulic system was installed.

About two production stations later, after the hydraulic system had been covered by plates, the radar equipment is being installed.

The radar installers did not know that a hydraulic system was under the plates, and were taking no pains to protect the system from damage. Sometimes they drilled right into the hydraulic system.

Spot the production problem here.

Write the production problem on the work sheet.

List the evidence.

Decide what action, training and other, is needed.

Observe each member individually. Coach where necessary. DO NOT talk to disturb the others. Make certain each column is correctly used by each individual. See guide for general outline of what should come out of this problem. Allow no more than 10 minutes for this. Watch for signs of finishing. Keep things moving. When most show evidence of being through, start the discussion.

Let's see what we have done with this problem.

Discuss with the group, calling on different members for their ideas on the various points. Remember, you are confined to the facts of the problem, but that each person is an individual and as such is entitled to vary his convictions as he sees fit.

If members lean toward the other action of moving one system or the other, remind them that two-thirds of the planes passed inspection. Therefore, the systems don't have to be changed.

If one or more seem hazy about the procedure to be followed with the work sheet, you may find it advisable to place a portion of it on the second board. Do not belabor this phase.

(For use with Step 1 of P.D. Method - Use card)

What is the Production Problem? _____ Leaks in hydraulic system

EVIDENCE	TRAINING ACTION NEEDED		OTHER ACTION NEEDED
	Training for Whom?	Training in What?	
One plane out of three rejected at final inspection because of leaks in hydraulic system			
Hydraulic installers experienced			
Hydraulic installation checked — no faulty work			
Radar equipment installed after hydraulic system covered by plates	Radar installers	Location of hydraulic system	
Radar installers not protecting hydraulic system — drill into it	Radar installers	Importance of hydraulic system	
		How to protect hydraulic system while installing radar	Put stop on drills?

"TACKLE ONE SPECIFIC NEED AT A TIME"

Are there any questions on this method of using the work sheet for Step 1 in this procedure?

1 hr.
to here Clear up remaining foggy points. Make sure each member has substantially the same work sheet as shown on guide.

Allow
20 min DEVELOPING SPECIFIC PLANS

1. The work sheet for Step 2 follows the same pattern we used when we discussed the Cost Records problem this morning.

Pass out blank work sheets for Step 2 and turn to second blackboard.

The first line after the heading is labeled "<u>What is the Specific Plan</u>?"

Here we write the name of the plan. In Step 1 we have considered the knowledge or skill needed by some specific people. We may combine several of those "Training in What" items into one plan—or we may break one down into several plans.

You recall that our card says, under Step 1 —

"Tackle One Specific Need at a Time."

What specific need shown in the column headed <u>Training in What</u> have you picked to work on?

The name you give that training plan is placed on the first line.

2. The second line, <u>Training for Whom,</u> will be the employees who need this training, as shown in Step 1.

3. <u>Training for how many</u> means the number of people to be trained.

4. <u>What content</u>—here you will list the items of training material to be used in the plan—the specific knowledge you want these people to have, the skills you want them to acquire.

This listing must be complete. Be specific—generalities are not enough.

<u>List just what you want them to learn.</u>

Go back to the evidence. Underlying causes must be remedied—list exactly the content to do that.

Clear up any questions on this column. Give examples—get examples from members.

Remember the rest of that item on the card—Who can help determine?

5. How Can It Be Done Best?

This column heading covers a large field in itself.

Here are some ideas which may be helpful in this connection.

Pass out Methods and Aids material.

Point out that the Methods can be used by anyone in any plant—the Aids will depend on what you need, what you have or can have.

Tell members that the material on conducting meetings will be taken up another day.

To the extent appropriate, review Job Instruction, stressing breakdowns and 4 steps.

6. Who Will Train or Help?

Pick individuals who are already prepared for this work or who can be coached.

Give and get examples of this.

When?—How Long?

Add the number per group in this column if the number to be trained is to be broken up.

Check against evidence for importance of problem in relation to time it takes.

Where?

Here, too, be specific.

Check against the evidence for wise choice of place.

Avoid using a meeting room just because a meeting room is available. Perhaps other places would be more effective for some kinds of training. On the other hand, if the shop is noisy and a machine can be put in an empty room, consider that.

Be certain every member understands the columns.

9. The last line on our work sheet is "What is the relation of this plan to other current training plans and programs?"

What priority should be assigned to this plan? Consider the importance of the evidence. Look at the strategy involved.

(For use with Step 2 of P.D. Method - Use card)

What is the Specific Plan? _____ Protection of Hydraulic System
Training for Whom? _____ Radar Installers _____ Training for How Many? _____ 20

What Content?	How Can It Be Done Best?	Who Will Train or Help?	When? How Long?	Where?
Importance of protecting hydraulic system			1 1/2 hours tomorrow, 20 in group	General Foreman's office
Importance of hydraulic system to pilot and crew	Explanation	Test pilot		
Cost of repairing damaged hydraulic system	Analysis of cost figures	General Foreman		
Location of hydraulic system	Cutaways — explanation	General Foreman		
Drilling holes for radar installation	Demonstration — practice	General Foreman	1/2 hour each man, schedule immediately, complete in 3 days	On job
Placement of holes Depth of drilling — 1/8"				

What is the Relation of this Plan to Other Current Training Plans and Programs? _____ Will take only 2 hours of each operator's time, and 10 hours of radar supervisor's time — less time than to repair one damaged hydraulic system.

28

DRILL PROBLEMS ON WORK SHEET FOR STEP 2

Let's see if we can use this form.

1. Do you all have the Step 1 work sheets you prepared on the Defective Hydraulics problem?

Review evidence column.

This points clearly to a training plan for the radar installers—they have to know the importance of the hydraulic system, where it is located, and how to protect it.

Will you make out a Step 2 work sheet for what could be done for just 20 radar installers. Now you may not know anything about hydraulics or radar, but we are not trying to develop a training plan. We are just checking understanding of this work sheet because it is a tool you will use when you go to work on a problem.

Have members work individually. The attached Step 2 work sheet is for your use in questioning, but no attempt is to be made to get individuals to have their work sheets conform with this sample. Discuss. Ask a specific member what evidence led him to put in a specific item of content. Use Methods and Aids bulletin. Summarize from guide.

2. Now we will run through the work sheet on the Disinfectant Reprocessing problem. This work sheet pointed to a need for training of both supervisors and operators.

All of us will work on <u>how the supervisors can learn to estimate needs</u>. Make out a work sheet for 5 supervisors.

Have members work individually, then tell you what to put on blackboard. Attached sample gives possible material—do not attempt to force group to bring out this exact wording. (Step 1 of this problem is already on one board.)

Point out that, in order to sell the supervisors on the necessity of estimating needs, they must have some knowledge of the product they are working on, and therefore, all the supervisory needs in the "training in what" column have been covered. If appropriate, tie into Job Instruction Step 1.

2 hrs.
to here

Take 10-minute intermission.

(For use with Step 2 of P.D. Method - Use card)

What is the Specific Plan? _____ Estimating needs for disinfectant packaging

Training for Whom? _____ Supervisor's of disinfectant packaging department   Training for How Many? __5__

What Content?	How Can It Be Done Best?	Who Will Train or Help?	When? How Long?	Where?
Use of disinfectant by Marine Corp	Explanation — pictures	Sales Manager *	Next Monday 15 minutes	Conference room
Properties of disinfectants	Demonstration	Chief Chemist	15 minutes	
Estimating needs Size of contract Production capacity Disinfectant powder needed	Explanation Discussion of work standards Discussion of schedules Blow-ups	General Foreman	1 1/2 hours	
		* Or a Procurement Officer or a Veteran		

What is the Relation of this Plan to Other Current Training Plans and Programs? _____ Training is so short — can be worked in without interference.

GETTING A PLAN INTO ACTION AND CHECKING RESULTS

1. There are no work sheets for Steps 3 and 4.

What is the Relation of this Plan to Other Current Training Plans and Programs?

Local conditions in your plant will determine what you must write down in these steps.

You will make written notes for these steps.

2. In connection with Step 3, we have a bulletin which may be of some help to you.

Pass out copies of "How to Launch a Plant Training Program" and read main headings.

Discuss the following ideas with the group. Get evidence of concrete thinking from them.

Does the training director's responsibility end when he has spotted a need and made a plan to meet it?

He still has to get acceptance and understanding, see that those who do the training are equipped, that the training actually gets started, and, of course, check the results.

Stress the fact that the card gives definite procedure to follow in getting a plan into action.

The training director has been working within the line organization—perhaps with top management and with lower levels of supervision.

He has been working on a <u>production</u> problem, he has used <u>production</u> records, talked with <u>production</u> people, when he identified the needs for training.

When he planned the content, he probably got help from the line organization and staff departments.

Emphasize that Step 3 may be the first time that he has discussed the whole problem and his approach with someone high enough in the line organization to give authority to proceed.

The evidence, causes, and needs which the training director located as he worked through the first step of the P.D. method give him his talking points for selling management.

In general, top managers are more interested in production facts and figures than they are in training techniques. Too much detail on methods may be confusing.

The training director must be ready to explain the plan—or help someone else—to middle management and all those who are affected.

He must be ready to arrange for the training of those who do the actual instruction. The time that this takes must be considered in making the training timetable.

The plan is not ready to "go into action" until an agreement has been reached as to who is responsible for making continuing use until the production problem has been solved.

Finally, when the plan is started, it must have management's known backing. The means may differ—meetings, announcements, letters—but this participation in the plan as a way to improve production is essential to getting action that produces results.

Be certain that each member understands the importance of getting a plan into action.

Suggest members read the whole bulletin thoughtfully and completely after the session.

3. The training director uses a 4-step method. His job is not finished just because the training is started—or even when training session are concluded.

Refer to card.

He must see what the results were—check them against the evidence.

Management must be informed of results.

These points check the training director's results as a plan designer.

If a plan is not getting results, he must find out why. Was the plan followed? Were the instructors competent? Did management back it? Did the need change? Has anything else happened to affect the situation?

Checking results is necessary because of the specific needs which are involved in the particular plan.

If one plan fails, it becomes harder for the training director to launch his next one. It is harder to sell management, and production people may be reluctant to spend time on what they may think is "just another kind of training."

Getting results is what the training director has virtually guaranteed to management—and also the most important thing he can do to establish his own plant reputation.

The training director must be the most severe critic of training that there is in the plant. He will be helped if management demands to be informed of results.

Even if the production organization is not expecting to be shown, the training director still must find out just what effect the use of his plan has had on the production problem.

Sometimes events in the plant mean that a plan has to be changed—perhaps while it is in operation. An engineer can repair a bridge while the train runs over it.

Training can outlive its usefulness. Remember that, while education is for the good of the individual, training is for the good of the plant and of production.

Individual gains and personal appreciation are by-products.

If the need for the training has ended, the training director should be the first one to recognize that fact.

Occasionally the need for the training ceases abruptly—the training director should be the one to see that a plan which is not needed is chopped off.

His final check of results, of course, is:

★ Is the plan helping production?

At the bottom of the card is the statement on line and staff responsibility for training results. Remember that:

★ The LINE organization has the responsibility for making
★ continuing use of the knowledge and skills acquired
★ through training as a regular part of the operating job.

But this does not relieve the training man of responsibility for:

★ The STAFF provides technical "know-how" on techniques
★ by which the line organization keeps a program in use as
★ long as it is needed in order to get continuing results.

T.W.I. has prepared a bulletin on how a plant can get continuing results.

> Distribute copies.

Let's look at the main headings now. You can read it thoroughly later.

Discuss the bulletin as follows, enlarging where appropriate.

There are certain fundamentals for getting continuing results.

1. Assign responsibility.
2. Get adequate coverage.
3. Provide for coaching.
4. Report results to management and give credit.

These items give a basic pattern for you to follow to get continuing results from any training plan you develop for your plant.

The item "Provide for coaching" is illustrated by five steps developed by T.W.I. for coaching in the skills of supervision.

1. Give reasons and advantages.
2. Get understanding of principles.
3. Select a problem and work it together.
4. Ask him to work out another problem alone.
5. Give credit.

2 hrs.
40 min
to here

Amplify briefly.

Allow
30 min

DRILL ON STEPS 3 AND 4 OF 4-STEP METHOD

1. Each of you will now make notes on Steps 3 and 4 of this Disinfectant Reprocessing problem.

Steps 1 and 2 are on board, and all members have filled in work sheets.

Use your cards to outline Steps 3 and 4.

Be specific. Work individually.

Discuss the various ways the different members planned to use Steps 3 and 4. Make it "live."

Emphasize that when the plan is discussed with management— it may be revised. You may have to go back and do more work on Step 2. You may even have to get more evidence.

3 hrs.
10 min
to here

If necessary, work Steps 3 and 4 of Defective Hydraulics problem.

ASSIGNMENT FOR SECOND DAY

1. When you go back to your own plant at the end of this section of the Institute, you will get to work using the 4-step method on a problem in your own plant.

Before then, we want to make sure that we have clearly established the use of the method.

★ Now you know you cannot spot production problems or
★ plan training in a conference. You cannot plan training
★ in your office. You have to get into the plant.

★ But I will ask you to check your understanding of the
★ method between now and tomorrow morning by
★ going through the four steps on a practice problem.

Suppose that, when you return to your plant, you find that your plant has suddenly been given a release on civilian production or received a new war contract; that not more than 200 workers will be involved, and that the change will happen in four weeks.

What will this mean in your plant?

It will mean something different in every plant.

Go into detail as necessary.

To a plant which receives a contract for a new war product or has to change its manufacturing procedures, this probably will mean that there will be no one in the plant who knows the new work.

To a plant which has been converted to war work, it may mean reconverting a part of the plant. But reconversion is not always simple—will your plant go back to exactly the same design as before the war? Are there skilled workers? How about supervisors?

If a plant has been built in wartime there may not be a supervisor or worker who knows how to make the new product.

Perhaps you already are on civilian production and this expansion is the result of a lifted employment ceiling to take care of new orders. Or perhaps raw materials have been scarce—now you can get more. At any rate, the plant is putting 200 workers (present or new employees) on this job. How about supervisors?

Relate this to each member's own plant as far as possible.

Apply this to your own plant—what would this change affecting not more than 200 workers in four weeks mean in your plant?

Use actual conditions in your plant right now.

Consider a change that is possible or probable.

Plan what could be done about it in four weeks.

Restrict your plan to what affects 200 workers or less.

Work through all four steps.

There are work sheets here for Steps 1 and 2. Make definite written plans for Steps 3 and 4.

Keep it simple.

All of you are to bring a complete 4-step plan tomorrow.

Remember that in Step 1 you often spot many training needs. But you can tackle only one at a time. Take just one training need and develop the other three steps for it.

If there are questions, clarify individually in terms of the specific plant.

2. Summarize on board:

Use present conditions in your plant.

A change in product, production method, or service in your company's plant or establishment.

Your plant must be ready to meet a problem which could occur within four weeks.

Not more than 200 present or new workers will be directly involved in the change.

3. Remember, this is still just practice—you won't do overnight planning at home on a real problem.

3 hrs.
30 min
to here

4. Distribute blank work sheets.

*Allow
10 min*

REVIEW 4-STEP METHOD

Express satisfaction as to group attendance and participation in previous session.

Quickly discuss the objectives of each step. Use different individuals for comment as you work through the 4-step method. Make this review snappy but thorough.

First, we must:

1. Spot a Production Problem.

We can't just say: "We need some training." It isn't even enough to go as far as: "We ought to do something about our supervisors."

We have to have a specific Why for training.

Why do we need to train?
Who are we going to train?
What is our goal?

We can get at these specific needs if we do some of these things under Step 1.

Ask one member to read aloud the first subhead under Step 1.

Get supervisors and workers to tell about their current problem.

Then and only then are we tapping one of the best sources of evidence for production problems.

Ask one member to read aloud the second subhead under Step 1.

Uncover problems by reviewing records—performance, cost, turnover, rejects, accidents.

Individual performance as well as group records should be reviewed.

Waste, scrap, and salvage records are important.

Ask a member to read third subhead under Step 1.

Anticipate problems resulting from changes—organization, production, or policies.

We cannot afford to wait until —
new equipment is installed
new shifts report for work

We need to get in early on the training needs that come from organization, production, or other changes.

There are other ways by which you learn of training needs:

Customers may mention some.
Public opinion may point to some.

Next we:

Analyze this evidence.

In this way we can really see what action needs to be taken.

Identify training needed.

This is where we begin to work on solving the production problem through training.

Tackle one specific need at a time.

In order to do a good job we work on one specific need.

2. Develop a Specific Plan.

Ask member to read aloud all Step 2 subheads.

We develop a training plan by asking questions and answering them.

Who will be trained?
What content? Who can help determine?
How can it be done best?
Who should do the training?
When should it be done? How long will it take?
Where should it be done?

Remind members of Methods and Aids bulletin.

Making a training plan would not be too difficult if that were all we had to consider.

Anyone can find one piece of training that needs to be done and plan to meet it.

<u>Watch for relation of this plan to other current training plans and programs</u>.

One training plan cannot be adopted without thinking of the other training which is going on in the plant.

You may need to consider whether supervisors are already doing so much instructing that they have no time to supervise.

Perhaps conference rooms are used to capacity.

Maybe the training you have planned is not needed as badly as some other kind of training. You are really going to have to consider the relation of your plan to the overall training program.

3. <u>Get Plan Into Action</u>.

Read each subhead to group.

<u>Stress to management evidence of need—</u>
<u>use facts and figures</u>.
<u>Present the expected results</u>.
<u>Discuss plan—content and methods</u>.
<u>Submit timetable for plan</u>.
<u>Train those who do the training</u>.
<u>Secure understanding and acceptance by</u>
<u>those affected</u>.
<u>Fix responsibility for continued use</u>.

When you take the training plan to management, some changes may result.

Maybe you cannot get as much instruction time from supervisors as you had planned.

You may have to change the methods you planned.

You must end up with a plan which management will not only approve but will support and will follow up.

The training director is a staff man, and the training plan will get its best start if he is able to:

<u>Be sure management participates</u>.

4. <u>Check Results.</u>

> Read subheads under Step 4 and comment.

> > How can results be checked? Against what evidence?
> > What results will be looked for?
> > Is management being informed—how?
> > Is the plan being followed?
> > How is it being kept in use?
> > Are any changes necessary?
> > Is the plan helping production?

This card sets down the method we have been talking about—the way to <u>meet a training need in your plant</u>.

We will use it over and over in this Institute as we have yesterday.

> Encourage questions about meaning of Steps.

10 min
to here   When you go back into your plants or establishments you will use it to plan training to meet the needs of <u>your plants</u>.

Allow
2 hrs.
50 min   ASSIGNED PROBLEM

Ask one member to present the problem assigned at the last session. Follow standard procedure. Put Steps 1 and 2 on board, completely. Allow an average of 50 minutes. If a member has not followed the standard instructions, if he has not used actual present conditions, go on to another member. Tell him you will come back to him next time.

Have three members present plans during morning. Do not belabor the discussions. Take a 10-minute intermission halfway through the morning.

3 hrs.
to here   Stress after each presentation the necessity for being on the job when meeting a production problem through training. Stress that this is only <u>PRACTICE</u>.

Allow
10 min

APPLY 4-STEP METHOD TO DEVELOPMENT OF INDUCTION PLAN

Institute Conductor <u>presents</u> this section—the induction problem is <u>not</u> to be developed from group.

1. Now we're going to consider "induction." Many plants have found they need an induction plan. This has to be a program of their own.

When we say "induction" we mean:

Getting the new employee acquainted with the plant, or the old employee with a new department.

Breaking the ice for the newcomer.

Introducing "him" to the company—maybe "her" to industrial work.

★ "Job training" is not part of induction.

★ "Induction" is "learning the plant."

★ "Instruction" is "learning the job."

2. <u>Induction starts</u> after the employee is hired, or the old employee is transferred.

There are many things which come before induction—and they undoubtedly affect the new employee.

What the guard does at the gate, what happens in the employment department—these affect the new man. But they are <u>not</u> part of induction.

<u>Induction concerns employees</u>—not visitors or applicants.

The impression of anyone who comes to the plant is important, and it may present a training problem. But it is not induction.

<u>When does induction end?</u> Maybe it never does, but we have to have a common understanding. Let's talk just about the first month in the plant. Each of you will have to decide on the appropriate time for your own plant—it may be less than a month or more than a month.

3. Can we work out an induction plan here?

Not a standard one for all industry.

Induction is the introduction of a person to the very place where he is going to work.

Each induction plan is different—because of the plant—because of the people.

We are going to consider some common points from induction plans.

In your own plants you may want to see whether existing problems could be met through an induction plan.

4. What will you have to consider about your own plant?

Get discussion.

New one:	modern poor transportation not in full production
Converted:	makeshift crowded
Same product as usual:	but have to use new materials newcomers mix with oldtimers
Waste or safety:	materials are scarce processes introduce new hazards
Unusual security precautions:	Amy or Navy

5. Who are the new employees who are coming to your plant?

Older men	Negroes	Veterans
Women	Handicapped	Workers from other plants

Do not let this grow into "die-casting"—"all women are alike," etc. The emphasis here should be on change in the employee group.

6. What are these new people like?

Not a-like.
To all of them work and work place will be:

new
strange
perhaps disturbing

When you plan induction you must have the viewpoint of the new person. Short-service people often make up a higher percentage of your turnover.

What kind of impression do you want these new people to get? You want them to like the place, to want to stay, to fit-in quickly.

It does matter whether they get off to the right start. Some things they could "pick up." If you learn a rule by breaking it, you will remember it the next time, but is that the best way to learn?

Do you think the new person will become a good worker sooner if he knows his way around? Of course—then you have to see that he learns.

Information booklets have their place—motion pictures may help—but neither guarantees that the person learns and remembers.

Induction is not "exposure to information." It is a training job.

7. Here is a production problem from which one training director spotted a need for induction.

> In this plant production was only 80% of capacity, and the orders were on the basis of full capacity. The training director was at the plant superintendent's meeting where it was discussed. He said he felt the trouble was worn-out machinery and that had noticed at least one idle line in every department he walked through on his way to the meeting.

> The chief engineer said the machinery wasn't worn out, that people were sore because they hadn't had any raises and were just careless.

> The personnel director said there was still room for them to make more money since most of the plant was on piecework, and he thought the trouble was that new people didn't know how to do the work.

Now, do you think there's a production problem?

Get group agreement that the production problem is "Production down to 80%." Put on board.

Encourage group to see that there is no evidence—everyone saw the problem but each offered a different cause.

8. It looks as if everyone pointed to a cause that couldn't be traced to him, doesn't it? Let's see what happened next.

> It all ended with the superintendent's saying he wasn't trying to pin the blame on anyone—but why not find out, and do something about it?

> The training director picked up the ball from there. He stopped in a department and pointed to an idle line and said to the foreman, "How long will it take to get the

punch press fixed? Is the conveyor broken, too?"

The foreman said, "What is the matter with the punch press? It isn't down for repairs. I don't have enough people here at work today."

That gave the training director a jolt. He began to really look for the reasons behind idle machinery. He got the same story every place—not enough people at work.

Next he went into what was behind that "not enough people" remark. This is what he found out:

> Fill in evidence column as you talk—see blackboard guide.

- 1,000 jobs in plant

- Never more than 950 filled

- Never more than 900 at work any day

- Turnover 5% a month plant-wide

- Turnover 20% a month, less than 3 months' service

- Turnover 30% a month, third shift, under 3 months

- Absenteeism 5% a month plant-wide

- Absenteeism 15% a month, under 3 months approximately—same all shifts

- Averages 10 months to get up to guarantee on piece rate

- 90% of rejects from less than 6 months' service

Now he got all this evidence from reviewing records. He decided it was time to talk to some supervisors and to some workers—some workers who were frequent absentees, and to some who were sitting in the personnel office waiting for their final checks.

He got a lot more evidence:

(For use with Step 1 of P.D. Method - Use card)

What is the Production Problem? _____ Production down to 80%

| EVIDENCE | TRAINING ACTION NEEDED | | OTHER ACTION NEEDED |
	Training for Whom?	Training in What?	
1,000 jobs in plant			Investigation too long?
Never more than 950 filled			
Never more than 900 at work any one day	Every absentee	Importance of work	
Turnover 5% a month plant-wide			
Turnover 20% a month, less than 3 months' service			
Turnover 30% a month, third shift, under 3 months			
Absenteeism 5% a month plant-wide	Every absentee	Importance of work	
Absenteeism 15% a month, under 3 months' service, approximately same all shifts	All new people and present short service	Importance of work	
Average 10 months to get up to guarantee on piece rate	All new people and present short service	Work they are to do	
90% of rejects from less than 6 months' service	All new people and present short service	Work they are to do	

"TACKLE ONE SPECIFIC NEED AT A TIME"

45

(For use with Step 1 of P.D. Method - Use card)

What is the Production Problem? Production down to 80% (continued)

| EVIDENCE | TRAINING ACTION NEEDED | | OTHER ACTION NEEDED |
	Training for Whom?	Training in What?	
Quits			
Provoked discharges			See bus company
Transportation, third shift			
Didn't like jobs	All new people and present short service	Importance of work	
Didn't like supervisors	Supervisors	How to work with people	Better supervisory selection?
Thought work dangerous	All new people and present short service	Safe practices	Check safety equipment?
Didn't like pay	All new people and present short service	Work they are to do How to figure pay	
Absenteeism			
Didn't think work important	All new people and present short service	Importance of work	Hall displays of completed product, news pictures.
Looking for better job	All new people and present short service	Work they are to do Importance of work	Investigate provoked discharges?
Tired	All new people and present short service	Work they are to do	Any better methods?

"TACKLE ONE SPECIFIC NEED AT A TIME"

46

Add to evidence column as you talk.

Quits

> Provoked discharges
> Transportation for third shift
> Didn't like jobs
> Didn't like supervisors
> Thought work dangerous
> Didn't like pay

Absenteeism

> Didn't think work important
> Looking for better job
> Tired

When he had all this evidence, there was certainly a better basis for action than when the three staff men were shifting blame in the superintendent's meeting.

Let's follow his analysis of the evidence.

Control discussion. Blackboard work should be similar to guide. As necessary, say "This training director decided."

Do you notice how much more action came out of "underlying causes" than out of just plain "facts and figures"? We need both.

★ Underlying causes suggest action.
★ Facts and figures give us bench-marks when we check
★ results.

Now this training director that found much action was needed. He decided that the first step should be to get new employees off to a good start, and that a clean-up job on the others should be done as rapidly as possible.

Some of the other training needs concern supervisors, but his decision as to the place to start to work first is on the new employees.

9. The training director is now ready for Step 2. He called his plan "Induction" and it is for all new people, which meant 50 a month to him.

He considered the need of getting across to these new people some idea of the importance of their work. He realized that they were going to have to have better instruction in how to do the work, but that would be a separate plan.

He decided that, while they would be taught the safe way to work, something should be done about their feeling they were in danger.

There was dissatisfaction about pay—some could be traced to the fact that it took them so long to get to the place where they made more than the minimum. Could anyone be wondering about the difference between the $40 he was guaranteed and the $30 in his pay envelope if he didn't understand deductions?

In all, these people just didn't seem to think it was a good place to work. What could be done about that? There were many good things about the plant—it wouldn't hurt to point them out.

So he planned Induction. This is what he decided on.

Distribute copies of Induction Step 2 work sheets.
Read and discuss.

Remember that, in planning content of an induction program, we have to consider:

- What new <u>people need</u> to know.
- What new <u>people want</u> to know.
- What <u>plant wants</u> them to know.

How are they going to learn these things? It is not just a matter of providing information—instruction is necessary.

The supervisor is closest to the new employee. The supervisor is the one most affected when the new person falls down. He carries most of the load in this plan.

But, induction is a team job. Each person does what he can do best. The general superintendent can't stop to talk to each new person individually—he can talk to them as a group.

You will notice that this induction plan takes place at four different times. Altogether it takes less than 3 hours. Do you think it would be as effective to just put all this together on the new person's first half-day?

You don't "drench" people if you want them to learn. You put first things first. But you schedule all, so nothing will be overlooked.

This plan can be started at once. The other training needs we saw in Step 1 require that supervisors be trained in order to carry them out. But this one need not be delayed.

10. The training director has to get this plan into action. He uses the facts and figures he collected in Step 1.

He points out expected results—drop in absenteeism and turnover if:

workers feel at ease, like plant, know work is important, understand just where they stand, supervisors show interest in employees

(For use with Step 2 of P.D. Method - Use card)

What is the Specific Plan? _____ Induction

Training for Whom? _____ All new employees _____ Training for How Many? _____ 50 a month _____

What Content?	How Can It Be Done Best?	Who Will Train or Help?	When? How Long?	Where?
Company production — mobile mounts for rocket guns One of newest weapons decreased Infantry casualties	Show completed product Point out what employee will do		Individually as soon as new employee is brought to department	Supervisor's desk
Size of company orders — not up to full production	Sketch on paper how daily lag piles up			
How people learn jobs safety — first quality — second quantity — third, but very important — Army and your pay			If necessary to keep waiting, provide some employee magazines	
How pay is figured guaranteed minimum piece rate deductions	Figure with him at his own rate; stress advantages of beating guarantee Summarize deductions	Supervisor		
Company policies interest of employees "good place to work"	Mention company standing and attitude; tell him he will like plant			
Company rules Badges No smoking	Explain 2 rules, give rule book to take home and study; invite questions		30 minutes to 1 hour depending on employee	
Company facilities Lockers — showers Lunch Package passes Driving clubs (continued)	Take him to locker Arrange worker to take to lunch Does he need one now? Find out how he gets to work			

INDUCTION (continued)

What Content?	How Can It Be Done Best?	Who Will Train or Help?	When? How Long?	Where?
Detail on pay Minimum Piece rate Pay period — lag Deductions Withholding tax Social Security War bonds Union dues	Uses his daily time cards Figure with him what his pay envelope will contain Answer questions Show him how he can increase his pay — on job every day, increased production	Supervisor	Individually, day payroll is turned in, 30 minutes	Supervisor's desk
Detail on rules	Go through booklet — answer questions	Supervisor	Individually, end of first week — 15 minutes	Supervisor's desk
Official company welcome	Speech and rocket news reel	Plant Superintendent	End of month, all new employees, approximately 50 in group	Auditorium
Detail on facilities Recreation, sports Employee store Employee magazine	Explanation	Personnel Director		
Detail on vacations and pensions Eligibility dates Provisions	Explanation Distribute printed plans	Personnel Director	1 1/2 hours	

What is the Relation of this Plan to Other Current Training Plans and Programs? ___ This can and should be undertaken for all new employees as soon as they come to work: we should catch up on all short service employees as soon as possible. Other plans can't start until people are trained to handle. Supervisors can do this now. ___

Would it help to point out the actual dollar and cents cost of this turnover?

The boss may have some ideas of his own—he may want more evidence—he may suggest a change in the training plan. The four steps are so closely related that we some times have to go back to a step, then on again.

It is very important that this particular plan be launched through the line organization. It would be rather easy for a production man to think that a staff man was criticizing how he had inducted new people in the past. But if top management says "This is the way we're going to do it," that is different.

The training director wants the results of this plan checked—and he wants the operation of the plan checked.

11. I have been trying to do two things here:

> Open up the subject of induction—but it is not just something to undertake unless it is an actual "training action needed."

> Set a better example of the detail needed in both Step 1 and Step 2—when you work on your own real problems, you will be doing very exhaustive work.

12. T.W.I. has a bulletin called "Introducing the New Employee to the Job." It gives examples of how two companies have approached Induction.

The forms they use, the time periods covered—both differ from what we have discussed here. But both have the new person in mind, and both consider induction as a training job.

1 hr.
30 min
to here
When you use the P.D. 4-step method, if you spot a need for Induction—remember it is training, and remember the new person.

Take 10-minute intermission.

Allow
2 hrs.
ASSIGNED PROBLEMS

3 hrs.
40 min
to here
Handle three more problems—standard procedure.

SCHEDULE FOR THIRD DAY

Four remaining plans will be considered. Encourage those members to review their work sheets and notes in the light of the plans presented so far.

W.M.C. Chief of Training will outline available local public training services.

Group will have opportunity to discuss the conducting of plant meetings.

3 hrs.
45 min
to here

Distribute copies of "Introducing the New Employee to the Job."

THIRD DAY - MORNING

Allow
2 hrs.

ASSIGNED PROBLEMS

Handle three problems.

Take 10-minute intermission.

Allow
45 min.

WAR MANPOWER COMMISSION TRAINING SERVICES

W.M.C. Chief of Training outlines available public training services and answers questions.

2 hrs.
55 min
to here

See detailed outline in reference section.

THIRD DAY - AFTERNOON

Allow
30 min

PLANT MEETINGS—WHAT CAN BE DONE TO IMPROVE THEM

One of the most useful training methods is the <u>plant meeting</u>. Staff meetings are commonly held in many plants.

Meetings to acquaint employees of change in policies, regulations, etc., are often held. Discussion meetings are held for supervisors.

These and many other meetings are occurring in plants all over the country.

A tremendous financial and time investment is made in meetings.

Do your meetings get results? Probably some do and some don't. That's the usual experience. Some plant men say that meetings are a waste of time, that they don't get any place, that they take too long.

Let's be practical about this matter. Let's view a plant meeting as a device for aiding production.

Compare it to a machine. If a machine isn't producing up to standard, do you just throw it out? Not until you have asked a lot of questions about it.

First you determine if you really need the machine's output. If you do, you take the machine apart to find out what's wrong. Then you try to correct the trouble and get the machine back to standard production.

Why not apply this same logical approach to the meeting question? Think about your own plant.

1. Is There a Need for Meetings?

Are there a number of important factors on which you want to keep your supervisors informed? Items like:

production schedules	company policies
product changes	organization procedures
union agreements	rules and regulations

If so, plant meetings can do the job economically and effectively.

Of course, you can send out memorandums on these subjects; but will they fill the bill? Can a change of policy or wage rate that required hours of discussion to formulate be clearly described in one or two paragraphs?

If a supervisor misunderstands a detail, but acts on the basis of his interpretation, he may embarrass both himself and the company.

Presenting such vital material at a meeting gives the supervisors a chance to ask questions about points which are not clear to them.

On the other hand, do you like to consult with your foremen about licking a production problem, introducing a change, getting a new policy understood? Meetings can also be valuable aids in these situations.

On these latter problems, individual supervisors may help, but they will get better results if they pool their ideas. 10 or 15 foremen working together on a production problem will arrive at far better solutions than any one of them will develop alone.

What's Wrong With Our Present Meetings?

Meetings fail for the following causes:

- no reason for the meetings—rambling
- just lectures or arguments
- too much to cover
- bad surroundings, poor atmosphere, or poor set-up
- last too long—don't start and stop on time
- careless leadership

Fundamentally, isn't careless leadership at the root of most of these complaints? A capable leader who takes his responsibility seriously will see that such conditions do not arise.

It seems that our whole problem boils down to helping our supervisors run better plant meetings.

3. <u>How Can We Help Supervisors Run Better Meetings</u>?

As in every undertaking, the key to running successful meetings is thorough preparation. If the leader has prepared himself in advance a meeting is more likely to have good results.

Much has been written on the subject of how to prepare for and run a meeting. For convenience, here are the basic points to keep in mind.

The following can be discussed as written on the board. Abbreviate if necessary.

<u>Get ready</u>	<u>Define clearly just what you are trying to accomplish</u> List principal points to be covered Decide what to take along: samples, models, charts, reports Find suitable place—quiet, adequate light, sufficient room Check before meeting to be sure everything is ready
<u>Open the meeting</u>	Start on time <u>State clearly just what you are trying to accomplish</u> Find out what members of the group already know about the subject—fill in gaps
<u>Guide the discussion</u>	Question group and individuals (what, how, why, etc.) <u>Find out what is interfering with accomplishing the objective</u> Use reports, models, samples to get across ideas <u>Discuss possible solutions</u>
<u>Close the meeting</u>	<u>Make sure that there is a common understanding about "Who is going to do what, and when."</u> Finish on time

Stress underlined items as key points in conducting a meeting.

Of course, just having a 4-step plan does not insure the success of a meeting. One learns to run meetings by running meetings.

For this reason, some companies organize practice groups to permit their supervisors to improve their technique of handling meetings.

After a little practice, anyone who clearly knows the objective of his meeting, and who has a definite plan for reaching that objective, need never worry about the effectiveness of his meeting.

<table>
<tr><td>30 min
to here</td><td>Erase board work.</td></tr>
</table>

<table>
<tr><td>Allow
40 min.</td><td>ONE MEMBER'S PLAN</td></tr>
<tr><td>1 hr.
10 min
to here</td><td>Handle tenth member's plan. Follow standard procedure.</td></tr>
</table>

<table>
<tr><td>Allow
45 min</td><td>DESCRIPTION OF USE OF METHOD BEFORE REMAINDER OF INSTITUTE</td></tr>
</table>

1. In this Institute we have been demonstrating the use of the 4-step method. We have gone as far as we can in a conference. It is up to you now.

At the opening of the Institute we said we must locate the places or problems in our plants which need our attention first. And you'll have to go out into the plant to do this.

You are going to do that in your own plant. Then, you will go on to use the 4-step method of meeting production problems through training,

2. Just what are you going to do when you get back to your plants? How are you going to spot production problems?

Go around the group asking this question of each member. Make sure each member:

- understands
- intends to use the method and to return with a plan
- work on a real plan—an important one—one that can be worked on within time limits; get help from the line organization.

Stress differences between production problem and
    training problem.
Stress differences between plan and program.
Emphasize: tackle one thing at a time.
Tell Institute members you will check with each one in person
    or by phone—make schedule.
Plans will be presented in group
    no criticism of <u>what</u> you decided
    full discussion on <u>how</u> method was used

3. You will probably find several <u>needs</u>. Some of them will point to more than one kind of training.

Suppose you meet your boss and he asks you what you've gotten out of this?

> a method
> consideration of several kinds of training plans

You can tell him your real work will be in the plant.

After you spot a specific production problem in your plant and draft one training plan to meet a specific part of the problem, you will bring it back for the final two days of the Institute _____ and _____, beginning at _____ a.m.

Be sure to include all four steps in any plan you make.

You will have to develop your own work sheets for Steps 3 and 4.

Do <u>not</u> bring in a plan already in operation unless you have used the complete 4-step method and gone through the plan on that basis.

We will ask each of you to discuss your own specific training plan. In order that we can discuss it without any loss of time, will you put all four steps on large pieces of paper we can hang on the blackboard, or bring 6 or 7 copies so we can follow them?

If you do bring extra copies, they will be returned to you as, of course, they would not work in another plant.

1 hr 55 min. to here

Pass out "Management and Skilled Supervision," "Improving Supervisors' Knowledge of the Work," "Keeping Supervisors Informed about Their Responsibilities," and blank work sheets.

If members are not familiar with "Supervisors' Five Needs," outline briefly.

Point out that these may be helpful in working out their plans.

Allow
20 min

OPENING OF SESSION

Welcome Institute members briefly.

1. Each one of you will now present his <u>production problem</u>—anything which interferes with production.

And his <u>training plan</u>—an organized method of solving a specific part of a production problem.

You will tell us how it fits into the <u>training program</u>—a combination of training plans coordinated to meet the training needs caused by a specific production problem.

2. To get the most out of this 4-step method of meeting a production problem through training, you have to be able to do four things:

> In Step 1 you are a diagnostician.
> In Step 2 you are the plan designer.
> In Step 3 you have to be a salesman.
> Then in Step 4 you are a "checker-upper."

3. These four steps are closely related—you cannot design a good plan unless you really get evidence—so Step 2 depends on Step 1. You cannot get a plan into action unless you can show that your plan—Step 2—meets needs—Step 1.

20 min
to here

Therefore, Step 3 depends on Steps 1 and 2. Step 4 is a follow-up not of Step 3 alone—it means that you see whether the training action planned in Step 2 really met the problem spotted in Step 1.

Allow
2 hrs.
40 min

PRESENTATION OF MEMBERS' PLANS

3 hrs
to here

Handle two members' plans—not more than one hour and a quarter each—standard procedure—take 10-minute intermission in mid-morning.

*Allow
1 hr.*

SELECTING SUPERVISORS

This section is to be presented and discussed, not developed. Get agreement on points.

1. Training alone does not solve <u>all</u> production problems. In fact, some <u>other action</u> often must precede training action.

Managements have often found that supervisory training does not get results because of the caliber of the supervisors.

Some plants have supervisory selection plans—some have none—some pay attention to higher level supervisors but forget that job-setters may move up the supervisory ladder.

Good supervisors are vital to management. Good means of selecting supervisors are important to good relations with workers, supervisors, and the union.

Characteristics of a good selection plan are:

> ways to locate good men from the ranks
> definite way to measure all against the same standards
> judgment by more than one person

Let's take a look at the supervisors whom we are going to train. Many are new.

Where are these new supervisors coming from?

> Can't <u>hire</u> supervisors.
> Promoted from the ranks.

2. Does it make a difference who is picked out to become a supervisor?

Management depends on supervisors to get the work out. Other supervisors and staff men are held up in their work if some supervisors are not doing a good job.

Workers need and want good supervisors. Unions may criticize both poor supervisors and poor methods of choosing supervisors.

Is the training director concerned about those who are picked out to become supervisors? He will be concerned in their training. Much training time is lost by training wrong people.

About everybody in the plant is interested in the <u>quality</u> of supervisory selection. Do you now have a selection program for supervisors in your plant?

Does it go clear down the line to job-setters, leadmen? Don't some of them move up the supervisory ladder—become foremen, etc?

Do you <u>need</u> a selection program? Deciding today that another supervisor is needed tomorrow doesn't give much chance for good selection.

In normal times, we knew workers pretty well—but now we do not know people well enough to make spot decisions. Will just anybody be a good supervisor?

The best operator is not necessarily a good supervisor.
The man with the best personality will not necessarily be a good supervisor.
Not everybody wants to be a supervisor.
Not everybody can be a supervisor—can't stop "doing" and begin "directing."

3. How does supervisory selection tie up with the training director's job?

<u>Quality</u> of supervisory selection affects the training program.
Group judgment of supervisory prospects is better than individual selection—training director should be one of the selection group.

The training director, because of the effect on his job, may be the one to call to the attention of management the <u>need</u> for better supervisory selection.

When we analyze evidence in Step 1, we may spot "better supervisory selection" as "other action needed."

4. Before we start to work on what is going to be in a selection plan, we know we're going to have to have something which will be acceptable to:

>management
>present supervisors
>present workers
>union organization

What will get management acceptance?

A plan that:

>picks better men
>shakes good men loose from "indispensable"
>   operating jobs
>provides objective basis for judgment

What will supervisors support?

>way to get better subordinate supervisors
>removal of charges of favoritism

What will the workers expect from a supervisory selection plan?

> better supervisors
> a chance to be considered for promotion by a uniform,
>   fair basis of judgment

What will the union demand of the plan?

> openly explained
> judge each person according to same standards

These requirements boil down easily because they are not far apart.

5. T.W.I. was asked to help plants to find a better way to select supervisors. A method, drawn from industrial experience, was developed. It is described in detail in a bulletin we will give you.

6. The first step is to <u>get candidates</u>.

> Write headings on board, and first step.

Steps in Plan	How Can It Be Done Best?	Who Will Handle?
1. Get Candidates		

How are we going to spot the people among our present employees who look like good people to consider for supervisory jobs?

One way certainly is to <u>ask the present supervisors</u>.

> Explain that it will not affect their own jobs.
> Emphasize their responsibility for developing men.
> Mention advantage of having good subordinates.
> Discuss supervisory qualities.

Do some of your supervisors hold back names of their best operators because they think they can't replace them?

> Bring supervisors together in a group, and ask each one to submit the names of two or three best supervisory possibilities.

> No one will want to have it seem that his department has no good men.

You may want to explain your need for supervisors to everyone in the plant.

Let workers "nominate" themselves.
Let them nominate fellow workers.

You will need to explain the selection plan:

Be sure they understand that only a few can be promoted. But everyone will be considered.

Perhaps you will want to ask the union to make nominations.

Make sure that union members understand how the plan will operate:

help in getting nominations is welcome
actual decision will be made by management
any question of qualifications will be discussed with anyone concerned

Who is going to ask for nominations—perhaps the manager would be the best person.

Fill in Step 1.

Steps in Plan	How Can It Be Done Best?	Who Will Handle?
1. Get Candidates	Nominated by present supervisors Workers' nominations Union suggestions	Manager asks for nominations

7. The second step is a rough screening—the elimination of those who do not measure up against the first requirements. How do we do this?

The head of the selection committee—probably someone from the personnel department—discusses individually with each supervisor the following about each name he has presented:

Man's work record
How he gets along with other workmen
Any supervisory traits, such as ability to train new men
How he conducts himself on the job
Does he make suggestions?
What special training has he had?
Is he level-headed?
Is he willing to learn?
Is he acceptable to associates and supervisors?
Can he adapt himself to change?

When the supervisor considers these points, he may withdraw some of his nominations.

Similarly, union nominations are discussed with a union representative and the union may, upon consideration, withdraw names.

A man who nominated himself may withdraw his own name when he considers advantages, disadvantages, and responsibilities of a supervisory job.

Continue with blackboard work.

2. Rough screening	Discussion of each name with person making nomination	Chairman of selection committee

8. All the remaining candidates are then considered by a group.

Group can make better decision than any individual can.

Decisions improved.
Responsibility is shared.

Who should make up the group? Who is interested?

> Production department
> Personnel department
> Training department

One representative from each will make a good selection committee.

Group reviews all available records.

> Include health and safety records as well as production and pay reports.
> Use any ratings and test scores available.

If no one in group knows a man personally, an interview will be desirable.

Probably the size of the group of candidates will be considerably reduced by now.

If you have had some records—such as test scores—which give a concrete measure, and on the same basis for every person, you may have enough facts now to make a decision.

3. Consideration of all remaining candidates	Joint consideration in committee	Selection committee— production, personnel, training

9. If you do not have some standard measure for each person, some <u>practical test of ability</u>, you now proceed to get this kind of information.

Using the same measuring stick for all appeals to management:

> It gives a way to back up "merit."
> It decreases chances of favoritism.

A worker likes it:

> He has had his chance to try to make the grade.
> He can be shown where he falls in a group.

Unions approve:

> Favoritism is decreased.
> "Merit" can be measured.

What kind of "practical test of ability" satisfies these requirements?

T.W.I. recommends something simple and practical such as an arithmetic test.

> Every supervisor keeps some records.
> Answers questions about computing pay.
> Needs to understand simple directions.

Simple arithmetic tests are acceptable to workers and to unions, and management gets a measure of man's ability to read directions and do simple figuring.

Where do you get these tests?

> Many available commercially.
> T.W.I. provides sample of simple form.

How do you use these tests?

> Explain completely to all concerned.
> Best handled in a group so all get the same story first-hand.
> Give the test without a time limit, but record the time taken.

Continue with blackboard work.

4. Practical test of ability	Explained and given to all remaining candidates at once	Manager will explain

10. The selection committee is now ready to again review <u>the records</u>. The results on the arithmetic test are just more facts.

Should a minimum score be set?

> No, there is no "passing grade." This is just a way to spot the men who are <u>best able</u> to understand written directions and perform simple computations.

Do not let anyone make a decision solely on the basis of a test record. It is only one in the series of facts which must be weighed.

All the facts are now in; the selection committee is ready to consider each man on the basis of:

> Record and experience at the plant
> Own qualities—characteristics and acceptability
> Standing on a uniform test of ability

Continue with blackboard work.

5. Review of records	Includes personnel records and test score	Selection committee

11. The selection committee now makes its decision.

Each man must be accepted or rejected.

If the man is accepted:

> He may be appointed now.
> He may be put in a pre-supervisory training program.
> He may become part of a supervisor reserve or pool (but do not put any man in the pool whom you would not be willing to appoint tomorrow if there were an opening—in other words, this must not become an alibi).

Each person who knew he was being considered must now be notified. Do not hedge.

6. Decision   Appoint, reject, or   Selection committee
put in supervisory
pool

12. Would this selection plan work in your plant? All plants are different—you would have to consider what your plant needs, what you can sell to management, and what you can operate.

Perhaps you have a standard employment test which makes a uniform measure available for any worker. Maybe in your plant you would not think it feasible to open supervisory nominations to the plant at large.

You will have to line up your own selection plan.

But remember these qualities of an effective selection program:

> Participation in nominations
> Group judgment
> Use of uniform, objective measure

And any plan will have to be followed up.

At the end of this session I will give you a bulletin summarizing this supervisory selection plan.

Steps in Plan	How Can It Be Done Best?	Who Will Handle?
1. Get Candidates	Nominated by present supervisors Workers' nominations Union suggestions	Manager asks for nominations
2. Rough screening	Discussion of each name with person making nomination	Chariman of selection committee
3. Consideration of all remaining candidates	Joint consideration in committee	Selection committee — production, person-nel, training
4. Practical test of ability	Explained and given to all remaining candidates at once	Manager will explain
5. Review of records	Includes personnel records and test score	Selection committee
6. Decision	Appoint, reject, or put in supervisory pool	Selection committee

*1 hr.
to here*

*Allow
2 hrs.
40 min*

PRESENTATION OF MEMBERS' PLANS

Handle three members' plans—average 50 minutes each—standard procedure—take 10-minute intermission in mid-af-ternoon.

*3 hrs.
40 min
to here*

Distribute copies of "How to Select New Supervisors."

Allow
1 hr.
40 min

PRESENTATION OF MEMBERS' PLANS

1 hr.
40 min
to here

Handle two plans.
Use standard procedure with special stress on Step 3.

Take 10-minute intermission.

Allow
20 min

CHECKING RESULTS

We have referred constantly to the 4-step method. This morning we have given particular attention to Step 3. Your boss <u>expects</u> to hear from you—that's your lead for Step 3.

But what about Step 4? Does anyone have any doubts about that step? Do you know how to check?

Discuss.

Stress:
  Use of Step 1 evidence
  Use of existing records—keep simple
  Use of "before" and "after" figures

2 hrs.
10 min
to here

Remember you check production results <u>and</u> program design. In production results, you look for both <u>immediate</u> and <u>long-term</u> results.

Allow
50 min

ONE MEMBER'S PLAN

Standard procedure. Give special emphasis to Step 4. Ask whether member has considered these steps in getting continuing results.

  1. Responsibility assigned
  2. Adequate coverage
  3. Provision for coaching
  4. Report of results and credit

3 hrs.
to here

Allow
1 hr.
40 min

PRESENTATION OF ONE MEMBERS' PLAN

1 hr.
40 min
to here

Standard procedure with special emphasis on Step 4.

Allow
10 min

RELATION OF PLANS AND PROGRAMS

Now we're going to place a little more emphasis on one line from Step 2. "Watch for relation of this plan to other current training plans and program."

Refer to a specific member's plan.

Can you start right away on this training plan you told us about?

When you analyzed your evidence in Step 1, you found several kinds of training action were needed.

Suppose we take another look at just why you chose the one you did to develop into a training plan right away.

Which need is the most pressing? Which is going to be the easiest to sell to management? To the line organization?

Will this training plan really accomplish something definite?

Do you have people trained to carry on this plan? Can you get them trained promptly?

Direct all questions first to the man, then to the group. Keep from lecturing.

Poor timing can spoil the best plan. If the supervisors in a department are now attending the 10-hour Job Instruction sessions, would it be a good idea to arrange for Job Methods next week?

Or, even if it were a quite different type of training plan, should you hesitate before you suggest keeping him off the job part of each day, continuously?

There is another angle of timing—perhaps there is no conflict as far as the people who are being trained are concerned—but how about the people who are doing the training?

Can you think of starting one plan without considering the demands being made on instructors?

On the other hand, there may be no training going on in a particular department. Is it therefore a "good time for some"? <u>Not unless it meets current needs</u>.

No training plan can get under way until the instructors are able to do the training and until any material and aids they need are prepared.

Likewise, physical facilities must be considered—is there conference space available? Can the training shop be used at this time?

Sometimes there is overlapping between plans. Can they be combined? At least we can see that the same person isn't scheduled for both.

Occasionally there are disagreements. If a new intensive plan for a specific technical subject is introduced, what does this do to the old, longer program which has a different approach—perhaps slightly different content?

If there is "just too much training going on," and the new plan is designed to meet an urgent need, what other plan or program can be eliminated or postponed?

The training director tackles one need at a time—but he constantly watches <u>all</u> the training going on in the plant for the inter-relationships.

1 hr.
to here

Training can cause much confusion <u>if</u> it is not organized—and you might kill the whole training program—lose support from the management and from the line organization—if you do not <u>integrate</u> your program according to plant <u>needs</u> and the current operating situation.

Take 10-minute intermission.

Allow
1 hr.

ONE MEMBER'S PLAN

Use standard procedure, stressing relation of four steps. Use every item on card, including "Line and Staff Responsibilities."

You need all the evidence:

2 hrs.
to here

1. to be sure you have all the facts
2. to suggest and support content
3. to sell plan
4. to check results

---

*Allow
only time
actually
needed

(not
more
than
45 min)*

SUMMARY AND CLOSING

1. Training accomplishes best results when an operating man considers it so much a part of daily operations that he sees that it is carried on in his department.

When line supervisors have this viewpoint, one training man is able to serve a large operating department or section.

The training man provides the technical "know-how"—operating men <u>do</u> the training.

There are, of course, emergency situations where pressure is so great that training cannot be carried on in a production department.

In other cases possible damage to material, or product, or machine, or accidents to workers might make it unwise to do initial training on the production line.

Again, there may be common training needs—such as clerical, instrument reading, use of small tools, etc.,—in more than one department which can be most economically met through centralized training.

Or, extreme noise may make a separate instruction shop more effective than training in the actual department.

In such cases training men may do the actual training. When this training is done in accordance with production needs, it is effective.

Providing the tools for meeting production problems is the training man's contribution to his plant and to the war effort.

Explain certification—when a 4-step plan is actually in operation.

2. Thank group for their participation.

Go around the group asking each for comments ABOUT THE METHOD and its use in his own company—NOT ABOUT THE INSTITUTE or the Institute Conductor.

3. Training Within Industry wants to keep in touch with each plant, each Institute member.

T.W.I. at all times acts as a clearing-house. Give us your good ideas so others can benefit. And we'll be able to make some others available to you.

<u>Remember</u> the 4-step method will help you to meet a production problem if you USE ALL FOUR STEPS.

71

PROCEDURES FOR SETTING UP A PROGRAM DEVELOPMENT INSTITUTE

An Institute is limited to 10 members. No visitors are admitted to the Institute for informational or promotional purposes. A certain variation in the members of any one Institute is desirable. This Institute will be useful to men from small plants, large plants, new plants, and converted plants. When appropriate, one T.W.I. staff member may attend.

Selecting Institute Members

Plants are invited to send representatives. Individual training or production men are not invited. The T.W.I. representative will call on a member of the plant's top management and extend the invitation to send a representative if there is a man who is functionally responsible for in-plant training. Management is promised at this time that its training man will come back with a specific plan for his own plant—not general information.

It is not necessary that the plant have a full-time training director, but the authority and responsibility for training must have been delegated to a specific person in order for the plant to be represented. The following questions may be asked in determining the proper representative to send:

> Does he have a part in deciding what training is needed in the plant?
> Will he plan induction of new employees?
> Is he going to plan training for instructors?
> Will he be responsible for planning a Supervisory Training Program?
> Is he going to have to organize an apprentice program?
> Will he be the contact man dealing with outside educational agencies?

If the plant has not assigned the responsibility for training to a specific person, this may result in a request for assistance in finding a training director. One way to get a training director is to hire one. Another and better way is to take a man from the line organization who knows the plant, and through such means as this Institute, help him with the technical side of his job. When an operating man has the responsibility for training as part of his job, but not a training title, he is, of course, eligible to attend the Institute.

If a T.W.I. visit results in the appointment of a training director who comes from the outside, it will probably be best for him to get some familiarity with the plant before being enrolled in a P.D. Institute.

In the case of a very large plant, where responsibility for training is broken down by departments, an Institute for members of just one plant may be desirable. Make sure that all are training designers, not just instructors. The top training man is asked to attend a previous standard Institute, in order that he can handle the coaching between the sections of the Institute and later follow-up.

It should not be assumed that no training is going on in a plant. This Institute is a work session for men from plants which already have training programs as well as for those which do not. It gives the experienced training man the opportunity to review his training program in the light of new pressures and the aids in training now available. It gives any training man practice in using a skill approach to meet production problems through training.

After management has designated the man to attend, the T.W.I. representative will, if possible, call on the training director and give him further information about this Institute which has the backing of his management. He should not be made to think that he has been ordered to attend. The objectives of the Institute and its time schedule should be explained.

Details of time and place should be confirmed in writing with both the management and the company representative. In-and-out attendance destroys the value for all members and is generally disturbing, so it must be understood in advance that the Institute is not a drop-in affair.

Scheduling the Institute

Five days are required for the Institute. It is desirable to schedule three consecutive days at the beginning of one week and two other consecutive days toward the end of the following week, in order to allow approximately five full days for the man to work on a plan in his own plant, and to permit the Institute Conductor to coach the members.

The P.D. program head should not attempt, normally, to handle more than one Institute per month, since he will be responsible for individual follow-up with Institute members.

The representative of the Bureau of Training should be notified in advance as to the date of the Institute in order to insure his presence at the needed point.

Supplies

Each district is responsible for preparing its own blank work sheets, and for ordering other supplies at least one month in advance.

Certification

Program Development certificates are awarded when a 4-step plan, developed by the Institute member, actually goes into operation. This should, if possible, be determined by a personal visit but, if necessary, plant management may be questioned by letter or telephone.

After the Institute is finished, the Program Development Institute Conductor will schedule his follow-up visits—to both the management and the training man. It is desirable that these calls be made no sooner than ten days after the close of the sessions and no longer than one month.

Spreading the P.D. Method

There are frequent requests for admission of more plant representatives to a P.D. Institute. Question whether these men really use all four steps—or do they just instruct? Or perhaps they are interested only in the analytical technique of Step 1. Spreading parts of the P.D. technique, if it meets a plant need, is legitimate work for the plant's P.D.-trained man.

Occasionally what is needed is understanding and acceptance of the P.D. method to the extent that the right person will be sent to the Institute and his later use of the method furthered. In such cases, the P.D. Institute Conductor should be ready to explain the P.D. approach at a management meeting.

STRATEGY OF THE INSTITUTE

Program Development is designed to give to the plant man, who has be given responsibility for the training function, a knowledge of a 4-step method of solving production problems through <u>training</u>. He will develop the skill of training design through use of the method. This is not a matter of title—a production executive who has part-time responsibility for planning training is eligible; a man who has a training title but is an instructor, not a designer of training, is not eligible.

The Program Development Manual

The Institute Conductor's manual outlines the five days of the Institute. No part of the Program Development Institute can be omitted, and no additional material is to be added. The Institute is designed to present the 4-step method in an effective, proven way. The addition of other ideas and techniques, though in themselves of value, is confusing and keeps the members from getting a clear idea of the 4-step method in the very intensive Institute schedule. There is a great deal of blackboard work specified in the manual—no further work on the board is to be done.

The Institute

Always review the one-page summary of Purpose and Emphasis before the Institute starts—and keep it in mind throughout.

The opening of the Institute by the District Representative is important. It should never be omitted at the district office headquarters. In other locations, the Resident Representative will introduce the Institute Conductor.

Members are asked to introduce themselves—they will be brief if the Institute Conductor has set that example. There is not much participation in the morning of the first day, and this opportunity for each one to talk is desirable.

The definitions save time and misunderstanding. They are presented, not developed. If there are members from non-manufacturing companies, special pains should be taken to clarify <u>their</u> organization's production.

The Cost Records problem is used to demonstrate the 4-step method. It is deliberately skeletonized to make the overall structure clear. Leading questions should be used to get some participation but Institute members are not expected to practice at this stage. The Institute Conductor "dribbles" the ball—keeps it moving, but does not give it to anyone else.

The afternoon of the first day is spent on a drill designed to give the members familiarity with the detailed work of each step, and the work sheets for Steps 1 and 2. This is not practice of the method—just drill on techniques. It is more effective to get several answers, then explain why a particular one was chosen, than to argue with a member about why his reply was "wrong."
There should be no argument about the scantiness of these

drill problems—members are not being asked to get evidence, merely to identify it. Since each item of evidence is analyzed separately, we look at this as "the part of the evidence that we have." Members should not be told to "think of their own plants" in Step 1—just use what is here. However, in Step 2, if a member asks about available space, the Institute Conductor may say, "Use what you would find in your plant."

The work on the overnight assignment is the first <u>real</u> use of the method. However, emphasize that it is practice, not problem-solving. Make sure that members understand that present conditions are to be actual conditions, and that the anticipated change is one which could reasonably happen.

Induction is presented as a subject on which T.W.I. has, in its clearing-house function, collected some useful information. It is not developed as a problem. Particularly when "induction programs are offered to industry" is it important to stress: designing an induction plan is an in-plant job, operation of the induction plan is a supervisory responsibility.

Plant meetings are discussed for their use as a training method.

Training Services are outlined by the Chief of Training. T.W.I. is responsible for giving adequate advance notice and for assisting the Chief of Training in making his section of the Manual effective.

At the end of the third day, several T.W.I. bulletins are distributed—not simply because they are available (T.W.I. has other good bulletins) but because they will provide specific information.

Remind members that, in thinking of their plant's problems when they are away from the plant, they have been looking at a plant problem through a telescope. When they get back to the plant they can look at a problem through a microscope.

The members present their plans to the group in order that:

> 1. Their understanding of the method can have a final check.

> 2. They will get experience in talking about evidence of the problem, a plan to overcome the underlying causes, the results that can be expected, and the way the results can be checked.

> 3. The group will get conviction of broad application of the method.

The plans are not considered as something to be re-made by the group. Institute members may question—and they and the man presenting the plan can take from the discussion whatever is of value and suitable to their individual plant situations. Neither the Institute Conductor nor members should "expert" a plan.
Taking copies of each others' plans should be discouraged as

it contradicts the basic P.D. philosophy of training that is tailor-made for individual specific needs.

Presentation of the plans is interspersed by a presentation in a field where T.W.I., in its clearing-house function, has gathered special information—Supervisory selection.

<u>P.D. Institutes for T.W.I. Staff Members</u>

In putting on a P.D. Institute for T.W.I. staff members, it is appropriate to assign to them, for overnight work at the end of the first day, a problem of getting continuing use of one of the T.W.I. supervisory programs in a plant where they know actual conditions, instead of using the usual problem about the "change in four weeks."

During the Institute interim each member should be required to work on a genuine problem of his own, directly part of his T.W.I. job. He must identify his production, spot a problem, get and analyze the evidence, develop a plan, sell it to the District Representative, and check the results. He will then, of course, be eligible for certification.

STANDARD PROCEDURE FOR HANDLING A PROBLEM AND PLAN

ACCORDING TO PROGRAM DEVELOPMENT 4-STEP METHOD

1. Ask Institute member to come to the head of the table and give the background for the problem he is going to describe and the plan he developed:

Picture of the situation
Stage where he got in on it, or
Why he started to dig in and spotted the problem

2. Ask member "What is the production problem?"

As necessary:	ask, "What is production?"
	refer to definition of production
	ask, "What is interfering with
	    production?"
	ask, "What are you trying to correct,
	    improve, or prevent?
	ask, "What is bothering the boss?"
	refer to definition of production problem

Avoid getting:	an objective—need to state problem
	    to get evidence
	mere statement of fact—must be an
	    interference
	training problem or his personal problem
	    (get: "20% of powder has to be
	    re-processed," rather than "to
	    decrease re-processing," or "to
	    save materials," "to improve use
	    of manpower.)

Write production problem on board.

Ask group members if they have any questions about production problem.

3. Ask member "What evidence is there that this is a problem?"

Sketch evidence column on board - fill in evidence.

As necessary:	say, "The production problem gives us a
	    general statement—what support-
	    ing, facts are there?"
	ask, "Why is this a problem?"
	ask, "What makes you know you have a
	    problem?"
	ask, "What are the facts in the situation?"
	ask, "What are the underlying causes of
	    this fact?
	    "What made this happen? Did it
	    happen just once?"
	ask, "Does this apply to all the people
	    (or in all departments, or on all
	    shifts)?"
	ask, "Can any of this be put in figures?"

Get people into evidence column.
Do not combine ideas in evidence—do not write "Supervisors and workers think job dangerous and dirty"—make four entries.

In anticipated problems, the reasons why a change is to take place are important evidence needed in designing content.

In anticipated problems it is important to include in evidence column the schedule that has to be met, any cost standards—the factual material that will be needed in Steps 3 and 4.

4. Ask member to take his P.D. card and tell how he used and what he got from:

> Get supervisors and workers to tell about their current
>   problems
> Uncover problems by reviewing records—
>   performance, cost, turnover, rejects, accidents
> Anticipate problems resulting from changes—
>   organization, production, or policies

Ask: "Does this suggest any more evidence?"

Stress as necessary: Use all three means of getting evidence on all problems.

> Supervisors present problems - workers' opinions,
>   review records, anticipate effect of change
> Records reveal-problems—get supervisors and
>   workers' opinions, effect of change
> Anticipated problem—supervisors and workers
>   opinions, records for similar problems or in
>   similar plants

5. Ask group members:

> Do you have any questions about:
>   way he used the method?
>   this evidence
>   underlying causes

> If you were in this man's shoes, would you want any
>   more evidence?

6. Ask member to refer to card (or "What is next in our method?")

> Ask, "How did you analyze this evidence?"
>   "What necessary action did you see?"
>   "Training for whom? In what? Other action?"

> Sketch column headings.

> Read first item of evidence—"Is there any training
>   action which would correct, improve or prevent?"

Stress: Training action needed—only working on training which is necessary because the facts of the situation demand it.

Say: "We have to identify the people who need training, and decide what we want them to know or learn to do."

Write the training action under "for whom," and "in what."

Ask, "Is any other action needed? Not action by you, necessarily—but action you will suggest either along with training action, or perhaps before training action can be taken. But don't use this as an alibi."

As appropriate, indicate that action does not stem out of all items of evidence. We collect all possible evidence before trying to analyze it. We analyze just one item of evidence at a time, but we analyze it in terms of all the evidence available. In the defective hydraulics problem, if we had not known that the system was all right immediately after it was installed, we might have considered training for the workers who installed the hydraulic system. But the other evidence ruled that out. That training was not needed.

Some of these facts will be important bench-marks for checking results in Step 4.

Illustrate from member's own problem.

Do not say: "This is just a fact and we can't do anything about it."

Repeat analysis of evidence and identification of action with each item of evidence. Having the same phrase repeated under "Training in what" has an effective impact.

Ask member: "Now that you have analyzed your evidence, are you satisfied that you have enough evidence to develop a training plan, to stress to management the need for action, and against which you can check results?"

As appropriate, say: "You may have to re-work Step 1 several times—organize a final work sheet."

7. Refer to card, "Tackle one specific need at a time."

Stress: There is work to do between preparing a Step 1 work sheet and a Step 2 work sheet.

This line on the card is our tie-in to Step 2. Several Step 2 plans can come from one Step 1. You identify a group of people who need exactly the same training. This may involve several needs you have noted under "Training in What."

You tackle "one specific need"—this means
a suitable grouping, to meet a part of
the production problem.

Emphasize: This does not mean that there can only be
one training plan in operation at one time
—but make your plans one at a time.

8. Refer to card.

Ask member: "What is the name of your plan?"
"Who will be trained? How many?"

Sketch these headings on board. Fill in.

Ask: "What is the first item of content you have planned?"
"The first thing you want these people to know or learn
to do?"

Stress: You have to re-work the Step 2 work sheet
several times. Eventually you will put it in
the order of what comes first, and next.

Refer to card. Ask, "Who can help determine content? Did you
have help? Do you need help?"

Sketch content heading—fill in first item.

As appropriate, point out relation of content to
underlying causes.

Refer to card—"How can it be done best?" Sketch column headings.

Ask member to tell you his plan.

As appropriate, ask group what two things must be
considered in planning "How"—methods
and aids. Refer to Methods and Aids bulletin.
Do not ask group to suggest methods or aids.

As appropriate, remind or ask member and group
about principles of good instruction—
breakdowns as an aid—4 steps of instruction
—Importance of practice if someone is to learn
to do something.

Fill in method and any aids.

Refer to card. Who will do the training?"

Stress: two things to watch—has to have the necessary
knowledge or skill—has to be able to instruct
— may have to help in on one or both—that is
a separate training, plan.

Stress: training is not just a technical job—who influences
these people—gets them to do things.

As appropriate: Point out that man who designed the plan is not doing the instructing.

Sketch column heading and fill in.

Refer to card. Sketch "When" column.

Ask member: "When will this training start?"
"How long will it take?"
"If in groups, how many in the group?"

Ask member: "In the light of your problem, is this much time justified? Is this enough time in view of the evidence of lacks that must be corrected? Is the amount of time appropriate for the method you have chosen? Is the number in the group suitable for the way you plan the training? Can the person who will do the training give this much time? Will he be prepared to do the training on this date?"

Fill in "When" column.

Refer to card. Ask member "Where will the training take place?"

As appropriate, remind member and group to consider importance of evidence (good setting may be needed), the method of training being used (machines may be needed for practice), the person who will do the training, the length of the training (perhaps a regular production line cannot be tied up that long or interrupted that often).

Fill in "Where" column.

Repeat with member for other items of content.

If length of time is great, total the hours, ask average payroll cost, ask if this ties in with evidence of need.

When plan seems too comprehensive, ask if all the people need this much knowledge or this degree of skill.

When the Step 2 plan is the T.W.I. Job Instruction plan, for example, all columns are still filled in—what is the content, how is it put across, etc?

9. Ask member: "What entries in the 'Training in What' column in your Step 1 did you use in designing this plan?"

"How did you cover the evidence in your content?"
"What did you do about this evidence?"
"What led you to put this content in?"

Stress: Content must come from evidence, but we use principles of good instruction—we try to get people interested in work before we instruct them in how to do it.

We do not plan training in Step 1—merely spot training needs. We do <u>design</u> training in Step 2.

As necessary, point out: When we are designing training, we may have to go back to Step 1 and get more evidence.

10. Ask group members to take cards and look at Step 2.

Say: "We are not designing his plan—we are interested in his use of the method."

"Do you understand how his content came from the evidence?"

"What about getting help in planning the content? The man who helps you plan the content will help you sell your plan."

"Are there any questions about the methods he plans to use? the aids? Remember the lacks he was trying to overcome—should these methods accomplish that?"

"Do you want to know why he chose the person he did to do the training?"

"Are there any questions about the time or the timing? the place?"

11. Ask member to refer to card. What is the relation of this plan to other current training plans and programs?"

Stress: "This is the link to Step 3. In view of the evidence and your plan to solve part of the problem, are you ready to go to management now? How will this fit in with other training? If it does not fit, is this more important?"

12. Ask member to read his written notes on Step 3.

Ask one group member: "How did he stress evidence? What facts and figures did he use?"

Point out: If you don't have evidence when you go to management, you may have to return to Step 1 and get it.

Ask another member: "What results did he say could be expected?"

Ask another member: "How did he talk about his plan? How far did he go into content and methods?"

Point out: This may mean revision of Step 2 plans.

Ask another member: "What about a timetable?"

(If member did, not have a timetable, ask him whether it will be important to schedule who will be trained, by what date.)

Ask member presenting plan: "Have you made or will you need to make a Step 2 plan for the person who does the training?" (Do not review this plan, however.)

Ask another member: "How is he going to get understanding and acceptance by those affected?"

Stress: This includes people being trained, their supervisors, those who will do the training.

As appropriate, discuss T.W.I. middle management philosophy.

Ask another member: "What was done about responsibility for continuing use?"

13. Ask member to summarize management participation in this plan.

Stress: evidence from management—Step 1
planning content—Step 2
responsibility for continuing use—Step 3
participation necessary in order to get results—
Step 4

Get understanding on difference between management participation and mere approval or sponsorship.

14. Ask member to read his written notes on Step 4.

Ask one group member: "How is he going to check results?"
"Against what evidence?"

Stress: "Unless we have specific evidence in Step 1, we are not in good position to plan content, to sell our plan to management, or to check results."

Ask another member: "What evidence of lacks can he refer to?"
"What improvements are expected?"

Ask another member: "How is management to be informed?"

Ask another member: "Do you understand how he will know whether the plan is being followed?"

Ask another member: "What is to be done to see that these people use what they have learned?"

Remind member presenting problem: "You will keep in touch with this to see if any changes are necessary.

Remind member that in Step 4 he both checks results and checks operation of his plan.

15. Refer to card. Stress to member that "Is the Plan Helping Production?" means "Has this eliminated the production problem or licked some of the difficulties listed under the evidence?"

COMMENTING AND DISCUSSION ARE ON USE OF THE METHOD, NOT ON THE PLAN ITSELF. GET PARTICIPATION, ACCEPTANCE, AND AGREEMENT—BUT DO NOT "EXPERT" THE PLAN. USE AND (IF NECESSARY) CLARIFY MEMBER'S OWN WORDS. KEEP DISCUSSION GOING WHILE DOING BLACKBOARD WORK.

Allow
45 min

WAR MANPOWER COMMISSION TRAINING SERVICES

30 minute presentation by Regional, State or Area Chief of Training followed by 15 minutest discussion—if no W.M.C. Training Representative can attend, the P.D. Institute Conductor is responsible for the presentation of a correct, <u>current</u> picture of <u>local</u> training services.

1. The primary objective of the training agencies is to increase war production.

There are W.M.C. training coordinators in every industrial area—their function and responsibility is to:

> provide service in accordance with local needs
> coordinate various training agencies—avoid
> > duplication

2. Since you have spent these three days analyzing production problems and discussing their solution through training, let me take a common type of production problem and illustrate what various training agencies can do to help you solve it.

Do you ever have any spoiled work—any scrap—any rejects—any re-work?

What is the cause of the spoiled work?

There may be several causes:

> Worker does not know how to do the job.
> Worker may not care about quality.
> Supervisor may be poor.
> Layout may be cause of poor work.
> Inspectors may reject acceptable work.
> Plant morale low.

Put in upper right hand corner of board, in skeleton form.

<u>Cause of Spoilage</u>
Worker untrained
Worker not interested
Poor supervision
Poor layout
Faulty inspection
Low morale

Any one of these may be the cause of the spoiled work—or there may be a combination of causes.

You probably can do something about every one of these causes.

You also can get help in getting at any one of these.

3. In this city there is a W.M.C. Area Training Council made up of representatives of all the federally financed war training agencies.

```
┌─────────────────┐              ══════════════════════
│ Put at top center│             Area Training Council
└─ of board        │             ══════════════════════
```

4. You are already familiar with Training Within Industry. The three supervisory programs are intensive and specific, designed to meet plant needs for giving to its supervisors skill in:

> instructing—through the Job Instruction program
> improving methods—through Job Methods
> working with people—through Job Relations

They do not pretend to cover any other fields than these three <u>skill</u> needs of supervisors.

```
┌─────────────┐
│ Add to      │
└─ boardwork  │
```

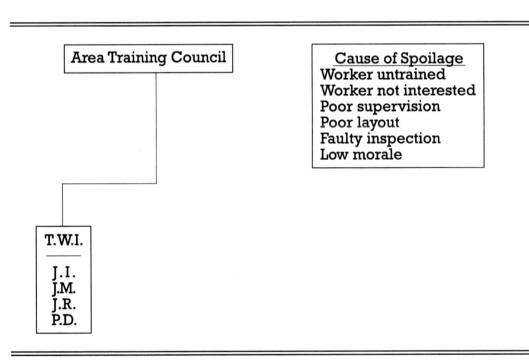

The fourth T.W.I. program is this Program Development Institute you are now attending.

5. The Apprentice Training Service provides technical and advisory assistance, but does not do any training or provide any standard training programs. It brings together the minds of employers and labor on training methods and techniques through management labor joint training committees.

The A.T.S. representative will work with you, in your plant, on problems connected with apprenticeship and with labor relations, as they affect training.

A.T.S. works with both labor and management in developing sound programs involving work experience and related education in order to provide all-round, skilled workers.

A special wartime service of A.T.S. is short-term training for specific mechanical skills.

A.T.S. representatives will assist with plant training surveys and will give counsel on such labor relations problems as trainee or apprentice wages.

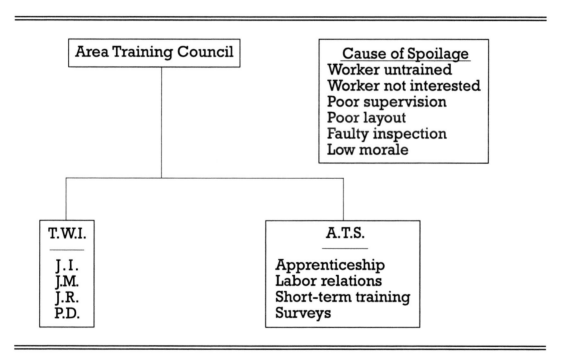

Give local examples.

6. The third of the training agencies is Vocational Training for War Production Workers. This is a national service available through the State Department of Education and the local public schools.

V.T.W.P.W. will help to prepare people to work in your plant:

> those you have placed on your payroll
> those who expect jobs after they have been trained.

V.T.W.P.W. will also help to increase the ability of your present employees through supplementary or related instruction.

These classes can be put on:

> in local trade schools
> at your plant

V.T.W.P.W. will also provide service for plant supervisors:

> in specific knowledge fields
> in the field of foremanship
> in conference leading

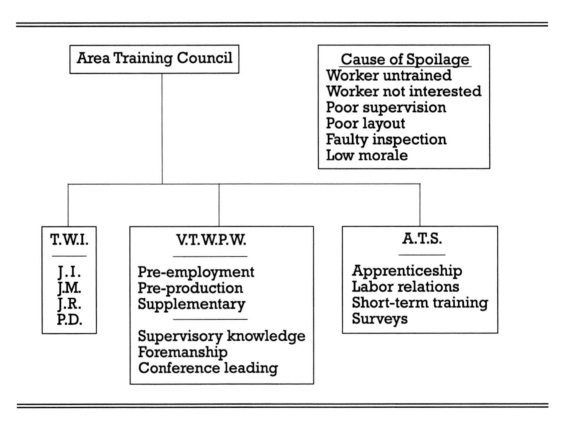

7. Engineering Science and Management War Training is the fourth type of training service. This operates through universities and colleges. (These courses are being withdrawn but in many localities there will be work at the college level.)

The training courses offered by E.S.M.W.T. are designed by a representative of the college working with representatives of one or more plants.

Their courses can be put on at the college or at your plant.

E.S.M.W.T. is designed to give the plant help when your plant needs people with:

> preparatory training in technical fields
> increased technical ability
> managerial training—such as industrial relations, production control, etc.

These courses are available for people whom a plant designates and also for those who anticipate employment or promotion.

> [Add to board work.]

Area Training Council		Cause of Spoilage

Cause of Spoilage
Worker untrained
Worker not interested
Poor supervision
Poor layout
Faulty inspection
Low morale

T.W.I.	V.T.W.P.W.	E.S.M.W.T.	A.T.S.
J.I. J.M. J.R. P.D.	Pre-employment Pre-production Supplementary Supervisory knowledge Foremanship Conference leading	Technical Managerial Preparatory Supplementary	Apprenticeship Labor relations Short-term training Surveys

> [Give local examples.]

8. Let us go back to our example of spoiled work and see how these <u>four</u> training services might help you get at the six causes we listed.

> [Put agency initials after each cause as discussed.]

We said that an <u>untrained worker</u> might be the cause of the problem. Perhaps a lathe hand who is experienced in working on copper or brass is now working on aluminum.

He simply needs instruction in how to work on the new metal.

The vocational school program—V.T.W.P.W.—can help you—in the school or in your plant.

Or T.W.I. will help you to assist your supervisors in how they can break in men on new work.

Perhaps the "untrained worker" does not mean merely a change in materials. Maybe some skilled craftsmen or highly skilled specialists are needed—A.T.S. will help you.

We mentioned <u>poor supervision</u>. T.W.I., E.S.M.W.T., and the vocational schools—all can give assistance in the field of supervision. That would have to be broken down further to see <u>just what you need</u>.

Then we come to <u>poor layout</u>. If you mean this in the engineering sense, E.S.M.W.T. can help you.

If you think of what the individual supervisor can do about the layout of his own work, T.W.I.'s Job Methods program may be what is needed.

We mentioned inspection. Both the vocational schools and the colleges are equipped to give courses in inspection training at various levels.

How about <u>low morale</u>? Supervision may be at fault. You may want to consider the Job Relations program. Perhaps an apprenticeship program would give an incentive to better work, or perhaps the labor organization in the plant does not understand what you are trying to do through training. The A.T.S. labor relations activity may help you on this.

9. You will have to determine the kind of training is needed in your plant.

We believe it will help you to know the training service available <u>without cost</u>.

This booklet describes the national W.M.C. training program, and these other pamphlets give you local information.

> Distribute "Blue Book" and list of names and addresses of training officials and other local materials. If time permits, discuss.

10. The plant training director has to <u>spot the basic causes</u> of production problems in his plant and <u>determine what training should be given, to whom</u>.

If you need bolts and screws in your plant, do you get a machine and make your own?

Not necessarily—if there is a good local supplier of bolts and screws.

And in training, you might well see what is available before you start to do the whole job yourself.

Of course you will have to:

> lay down the specifications
> arrange for delivery
> check to see whether specifications are met

It's just like buying the bolts and screws—we offer you a wide choice—<u>but there isn't any bill.</u>

11. Congress has provided these training services. Your taxes are paying for them.

Are you getting your money's worth?

> Not if you don't make your needs known.
> Not if you don't take advantage of what is available.

If you are in doubt as to which training agency can serve you best—let me help you. The Area Training Council will be glad to study your problem and make recommendations.

Completed Blackboard Work

Area Training Council		Cause of Spoilage	
		Worker untrained	VTWPW, TWI, ATS
		Worker not interested	
		Poor supervision	TWI, ESMWT, VTWPW
		Poor layout	ESMWT, TWI-JM
		Faulty inspection	VTWPW, ESMWT
		Low morale	TWI-JR, ATS

T.W.I.	V.T.W.P.W.	E.S.M.W.T.	A.T.S.
J.I.	Pre-employment	Technical	Apprenticeship
J.M.	Pre-production	Managerial	Labor relations
J.R.	Supplementary		Short-term training
P.D.		Preparatory	Surveys
	Supervisory knowledge	Supplementary	
	Foremanship		
	Conference leading		

12. Are there any questions?

Fifteen minutes should be allowed for this discussion.
Do not waste any time. If discussion is slow to start, give examples of training designed for specific plant needs.

Do not introduce another sample problem, but ask if any of the members have a problem of spoiled work—what are causes? Discuss training solutions, referring to outline of four services.

PLANT COACHING VISITS

Basic training in the Program Development 4-step method is given to a group in the Institute. If the Institute Conductor has given effective instruction in the first section of the Institute, it will not normally be necessary on coaching visits to give particular assistance on Steps 1 and 2. But it will be important to stress the planning of Steps 3 and 4.

On his coaching visit, the Institute Conductor checks understanding of the method, but does not attempt to pre-view the plan that will be presented in the second section of the Institute.

Ordinarily, one to two hours will be sufficient for this coaching visit. These brief visits are scheduled at the close of the first section of the Institute. This gives the Institute Conductor time enough to make a second visit to one or two members if necessary.

The Institute Conductor should not use the method _for_ the plant men. Except in unusual circumstances—such as to get experience for himself or possibly to sell an unconvinced member— he should not, for example, collect evidence by talking with the supervisors. His job is just to see that the plant man knows what to do and intends to do it.

The Institute Conductor will check to see that the man is working on one plan at a time. Occasionally he will find someone working on a plan to (1) train operators in new work. This may mean that (2) supervisors have to be trained in how to instruct and, therefore, that (3) someone in the plant has to become a Job Instruction Trainer, and that (4) a plant coach must be prepared. Therefore, _four_ plans are involved. Since all of this stems out of the _need_ for operators to learn new work, that is the Step 2 plan the training director takes to management in Step 3. He also must have his plans on the other three Step 2 plans because he needs those when he discusses "Train those who do the training." Normally there will not be time for him to present all four plans to the group in the P.D. Institute.

EVALUATION TECHNIQUES

(Introduce this material at any suitable time on fourth or fifth days in connection with a member's plan.)

Checking results is essential to successful operation of a training plan—it places training on an operating basis. It obtains management realization of training results and the effect of training on operations. Enthusiastic comments—superficial expressions of opinion from training directors, trainers and trainees—have often been accepted without insistence that such opinions be backed by objective or measurable results.

As management returns to a more "cost conscious" period, completion of a training plan will be followed by the preparation of a balance sheet. Management will recognize training as an operating function only when translated into production benefits. We cannot just think that these benefits result—we must show that a specific plan did produce them.

We must measure results in terms of evidence—facts, figures and percentages—rather than in opinion. Be sure to include the cost of the training in any cost figures you present. In determining the cost of a training plan, certain facts will be needed:

> Trainee cost—hourly rate x man hours involved
> Trainer cost—hourly rate x man hours involved

Your management would not approve this amount for a piece of machinery without wanting to know if it contributed to increased production, better quality product, or some direct benefits.

Checking results follows the same procedure in every situation. It involves:

> Compiling evidence on loss factors before training is undertaken.
> Compiling evidence on same factors after training has been given.
> Comparing before and after data..

Evidence on loss factors before training helps you to make adequate provision in the content of your plan to effect it.

Evidence on these same factors after training, and comparison with previous evidence, will help to determine the need for continuing the plan, the advisability of discontinuing it, and the need for improving the plan for more satisfactory results.

You will have to eliminate or gauge the influence of other concurrent factors.

When a new condition is encountered, and there are no "before" figures, or none available from industry averages, it may be advisable to set up a control experiment:

99

Select two groups of workers as nearly alike as industrial conditions will permit.

Make these groups as nearly identical as possible with but one exception—one is to be trained and the other to receive no training.

Control the conditions under which they will work, place on like operations, etc .

Determine factors to be measured. These factors must be identical for both groups.

Keep records for both groups for a like period.

Compare these records.

Repeat with two other matched groups until a trend has been established.

WAR MANPOWER COMMISSION

Bureau of Training

TRAINING WITHIN INDUSTRY SERVICE

PROGRAM DEVELOPMENT

*How to Meet a Production Problem
through Training*

1. SPOT A <u>PRODUCTION</u> PROBLEM

Get supervisors and workers to tell about
their current problems.

Uncover problems by reviewing
records — performance, cost, turnover,
rejects, accidents.

Anticipate problems resulting from
changes — organization, production, or
policies.

Analyze this evidence

Identify training needed.

Tackle One Specific Need at a Time.

2. DEVELOP A <u>SPECIFIC</u> PLAN

Who will be trained?

What content? Who can help determine?

How can it be done best?

Who should do the training?

When should it be done — how long will
it take?

Where should it be done?

***Watch for Relation of This Plan to Other
Current Training Plans and Programs.***

3.   GET A PLAN INTO <u>ACTION</u>

Stress to management evidence of
need—use facts and figures.
Present the expected results.
Discuss plan—content and methods.
Submit understanding and acceptance
by those affected.
Fix responsibility for continuing use.

Be Sure Management Participates.

4.   CHECK <u>RESULTS</u>

How can results be checked?
Against what evidence?
What results will be looked for?
Is management being informed—
how?
Isthe plan being followed?
How is it being kept in use?
Are any changes necessary?

Is the Plan Helping Production?

Responsibility for Training Results

The LINE organization has the responsibility
for making continuing use of the
knowledge and skills acquired through
training as a regular part of the operating
job.

The STAFF provides plans and technical
"know how", and does some things FOR
but usually works THROUGH the line
organization.

Publications from Enna

From Enna's new classics by Shigeo Shingo to our books and training packages regarding operational excellence, Enna provides companies with the foundation of knowledge and practical implementation ideas that will ensure your efforts to internalize process improvement. Reach your vision and mission with the expertise within these world-class texts. Call toll-free (866) 249-7348, visit us on the web at www.enna.com to order, or request our free product catalog.

Enjoy the rest of the books in our T.W.I. Training Series:

Job Instruction: Sessions Outline and Materials

Job Instruction, a short, intensive training program, was developed in order to provide skills in leadership to new and experienced supervisors alike. Contained within the Job Instruction book are samples, scenarios, and discussion topics which give you the tools necessary to properly instruct new workers and do away with waste and accidents, as well as cut down the time it takes to get a new worker 'up to speed' on his job.
ISBN 978-1-897363-92-8 | 2009 | $34.99 | Item: **922**

Job Methods: Sessions Outline and Materials

In teaching you the method behind the job and how to properly break down a job into its most fundamental parts, this book aims to teach you how to reduce wasteful behavior and wasteful steps within a job. The training material within provides you with worksheets, forms and sample scenarios to give you practice in scrutinizing and simplifying jobs.
ISBN 978-1-897363-93-5 | 2009 | $34.99 | Item: **923**

Job Relations: Sessions Outline and Materials

Job Relations was developed in order to provide management with a tool whereby supervisors could acquire skills in leadership. Contained within the Job Relations book are sample scenarios, discussion topics and instructional diagrams that relate the supervisor and his subordinates, show the dynamic of such a relationship and provide a way of looking at and dealing with these relationships that will benefit everyone in the company.
ISBN 978-1-897363-94-2 | 2009 | $34.99 | Item: **924**

Union Job Relations: Sessions Outline and Materials

Union Job Relations was developed concurrently with Job Relations in order to provide stewards with a way to acquire skills in leadership within their company and union. Contained within the Union Job Relations book are sample scenarios, discussion topics and instructional diagrams that relate the steward to his union, supervisors and the union members he is responsible for, shows the dynamic of such relationships and provide a way of looking at and dealing with these relationships that will benefit everyone in the company.
ISBN 978-1-897363-95-9 | 2009 | $34.99 | Item: **925**

To Order: Enna Corp., 1602 Carolina Street, Unit B3, Bellingham, WA 98229

Program Development Institute

The Program Development Institute was established in order to train people in setting up and implementing an entire training program within their company. Enclosed are worksheets, examples and practice problems to assist in developing the program as a training coordinator. With this book you will learn how to step back and look at the company as a whole, before implementing training and improvements.
ISBN 978-1-897363-96-6 | 2009 | $34.99 | Item: **926**

Problem Solving Training: Sessions Outline and Materials

The Problem Solving workbook instructs on how to properly Isolate, Breakdown, Question and Solve problems. From detailing just how you know you have a problem to charts and diagrams that will assist you in solving the problem, this book is a must read for anyone who deals with production on a daily basis.
ISBN 978-1-926537-00-9 | 2009 | $34.99 | Item: **927**

Bulletin Series

Based on the simple premise that in order to function there has to be an organized structure that recognizes that ongoing training is an investment that will always pay for itself the T.W.I. Bulletin Series is packed with ideas, concepts, and methods that will produce results. Contained within are bulletins that will assist in selecting supervisors, strengthening management and achieving continuous results.
ISBN 978-1-897363-91-1 | 2008 | $34.99 | Item: **914**

Other Books by Enna

Mistaken Kanbans

Let Mistaken Kanbans be your roadmap to guide you through the steps necessary to implement and successful Kanban System. This book will help you to not only understand the complexities of a Kanban System but gives you the tools necessary, and the guidance through real-life lessons learned, to avoid disastrous consequences related to the improper use of such systems.
ISBN 978-1-926537-10-8 | 2009 | $27.99 | Item: **919**

The Toyota Mindset

From the brilliant mind of a legend in the LEAN manufacturing world comes the reasoning behind the importance of using your intellect, challenging your workers and why continuous improvement is so important. For anyone who wishes to gain insight into how the Toyota Production System came to be or wants to know more about the person behind TPS this book is a must read!
ISBN 978-1-926537-11-5 | 2009 | $34.99 | Item: **920**

Phone: 1+ (360) 306-5369 **Fax:** (905) 481-0756 **Email:** info@enna.com

The Toyota Way in Sales and Marketing

Many companies today are trying to implement the ideas and principles of Lean into non-traditional environments, such as service centers, sales organizations and transactional environments. In this book Mr. Ishizaka provides insight on how to apply Lean operational principles and Kaizen to these dynamic and complicated environments.

ISBN 978-1-926537-08-5 | 2009 | $28.99 | Item: **918**

Training Packages

5S Training Package

Our 5S Solution Packages will help your company create a sustainable 5S program that will turn your shop floor around and put you ahead of the competition. All of the benefits that come from Lean Manufacturing are built upon a strong foundation of 5S. Enna's solution packages will show you how to implement and sustain an environment of continuous improvement.

Version 1: Sort, Straighten, Sweep, Standardize and Sustain
ISBN 978-0-973750-90-4 | 2005 | $429.99 | Item: **12**
Version 2: Sort, Set In Order, Shine, Standardize and Sustain
ISBN 978-1-897363-25-6 | 2006 | $429.99 | Item: **17**

Study Mission to Japan

We are excited to present an exclusive trip to the birthplace of Lean. We provide a one-week unique tour at a reasonable all-inclusive price that will guide you to a better understanding of Lean Manufacturing principles. Enna has exclusive access to Toyota and Toyota suppliers due to our publications of Dr. Shigeo Shingo's classic manuscripts. You will have one-on-one access to  Japanese Lean Executives and learn from their experiences and solutions. We also offer custom private tours for executive management teams over 12 people. Join us on our next tour by visiting www.enna.com/japantrip and register on-line or by telephone at: +1 (360) 306-5369

To Order:
Mail orders and checks to:
Enna Products Corporation
ATTN: Order Processing
1602 Carolina Street, Unit B3
Bellingham, WA 98229, USA
Phone: +1 (360) 306-5369 • Fax: (905) 481-0756
Email: info@enna.com

We accept checks and all major credit cards.
Notice: All prices are in US Dollars and are subject to change without notice.

To Order: Enna Corp., 1602 Carolina Street, Unit B3, Bellingham, WA 98229

CPSIA information can be obtained at www.ICGtesting.com
Printed in the USA
BVOW050410181012

303318BV00002B/2/P